Digital Executor®

UNRAVELING THE NEW PATH FOR ESTATE PLANNING

SHARON HARTUNG

◆ FriesenPress

Suite 300 - 990 Fort St
Victoria, BC, V8V 3K2
Canada

www.friesenpress.com

The intent of this book is simply to encourage the reader to consider the importance of a client's digital assets and associated requirements in the context of incapacity planning, estate planning, and estate administration. The author does not warrant or guarantee the accuracy or currency of any information provided herein. This book does not provide legal advice nor is it a substitute for legal advice. The laws in any jurisdiction are subject to change and are potentially different from what is presented here. The author is providing neither legal nor tax nor financial nor technical advice, and readers are encouraged to seek qualified advice from professionals in their jurisdiction for their specific situation.

Developmental editing by Victoria Gladwish
Copy editing by Adrineh Der-Boghossian
Front cover editing by Vincent Murakami

ISBN
978-1-03-911336-7 (Hardcover)
978-1-03-911335-0 (Paperback)
978-1-03-911337-4 (eBook)

1. BUSINESS & ECONOMICS, FINANCE, WEALTH MANAGEMENT

Distributed to the trade by The Ingram Book Company

This book is dedicated to my brother Paul –

You tinkered away, sorting out our IT at home, at work, and in the community. We are grateful to you for teaching us how to use tech to connect people, create conversations that build relationships, helping us laugh along the way.

Table of Contents

Preface

Some of us may not have had a digital life before the pandemic, but we all have one now. A digital life means a digital footprint and eventually a digital estate. Digital assets may simply be electronic records, but they are now the digital gateway to your clients' entire lives, estates, and legacy. This inference will have a material impact on the entire estate industry and the role of every advisor. The estate industry is not the only sector about to be impacted by the proverbial digital bus—every organization, business, tech company, tech entrepreneur, and service provider that engages online with consumers and the marketplace is affected by the digital tsunami.

Digital assets are our memories, our money, and our records. They are just now in digital form instead of paper. Simply put, they are electronic records, including the obvious things—our e-mail, social media, digital photos, gaming accounts, and household management accounts. We no longer have physical photo albums, instead our photos are in the cloud or stored on our devices. The not-so-obvious things—our loyalty points, reward points, community platforms, cloud accounts, video channels, online hobby accounts, cryptocurrencies, cryptoassets, digital collectables, non-fungible tokens (NFTs), and entertainment accounts are also electronic records, all part of our growing digital asset portfolios.

The concept of digital assets is not new, but when we consider digitization of our memories, our money, and our records, we can now imagine the valuation and sentimentality of those assets. Digital assets emerged with the advent of the information age, but ours will be the first generation to consider our online lives and digital footprint when declaring our wishes and preferences for our beneficiaries. Within the context of the estate industry, this assertion has an implication for estate planning, incapacity planning, and eventually estate administration. But within the broader global economy, this statement has an implication for every entity that deals with individuals digitally or online, regardless of the size of the client's footprint or the degree of monetized value of the client's portfolio.

Estate planning of our digital lives is a new aspect of will and estate planning, incapacity planning, and estate administration, resulting in implications for all aspects of our online lives. Just as a business may engage with an executor or fiduciary to shut down or address a deceased client's subscription or account (of a physical newspaper, magazine, or home utility), so too will entities need to address both client wishes and subsequent fiduciary inquiries about shutting down the online lives of deceased individuals.

All businesses and organizations, from the local coffee shop to a non-profit or a globally integrated complex enterprise, will need to consider how they will handle their clients' digital accounts in terms of how they are closed down, sunset, memorialized, or transferred to the fiduciary and/or beneficiaries. If you engage with clients through e-mail, offer loyalty points or rewards, or retain client information or data online, you too are implicated and will need to consider your policy and terms of service in dealing with clients and their fiduciaries during incapacity and/or death.

Understanding and addressing a client's digital assets isn't about "solving" digital assets with a snappy list of things the client should do or a cleverly written policy statement. Digital assets are pervasive in various forms in your clients' lives, and organizational processes, practices, and tools will most likely need updating to address them. Digital assets are not only assets unto themselves, but also manifestations of physical things, often providing the conduit or access to underlying already intangible assets.

We are also on the doorstep of electronic wills, which are digital assets unto themselves, representing the tip of the industry's transformation that will quietly drive a wave of digitization throughout the entire estate industry. Watch as the entire end-to-end processes of estate planning and administration and the associated businesses connect and electrify as a result. Estate advisors must now be digital estate advisors using updated estate planning techniques, organizational practices, and tools to deal with a digitally savvy and connected client. Are organizations, businesses, and service providers ready for their customer service phone lines to be flooded by a whole new type of stakeholder, including fiduciaries, estate advisors, estate lawyers, and beneficiaries looking for a deceased person's digital assets?

This book is a primer for understanding a client's personal user context in navigating estate management in the digital age with introductions to technology and the underlying practical aspects and differentiation between digital asset classes. Not all digital assets are the same, with nuance and application positioned in the broader context of digitization of the industry. Social media, e-mail, digital photos, and other familiar digital assets represent a rudimentary beginning, and if we think the pandemic accelerated digital adoption, wait until electronic will legislation becomes widespread. Electronic wills are at the apex of the digitization of the estate industry, and this notion alone will drive broader industry disruption.

Estate advisors, and their respective organizations and professions have work to do in updating policies, practices, procedures, and tools to address an individual client's digital assets in estate planning, incapacity planning, and estate administration. Online businesses, service providers, and tech companies also need to consider that clients will have expectations, preferences, and estate requirements in the management of their account data or digital assets both during life, and if they lose capacity, and when they pass away. Businesses, regardless of size and type, will also need to establish policies for business continuity, business transition, and succession planning for their digital assets, but the focus of this book is on digital assets owned by an individual client, providing basic awareness from a tech management perspective for one's personal digital footprint.

From an estate industry context, today's executor is a digital executor—as such, today's estate advisor must be a digital estate advisor. Cracking the code to digital death and its afterlife requires deciphering the technical management aspects of these new assets. If nothing else, advisors need to understand basic user perspectives and the application of technology in our day-to-day lives, but moreover, when to engage a technical professional. Online businesses, service providers, and technology companies need to begin their awareness journey to understand the expectations users have with respect to their digital lives upon death.

Using this book as an introduction to digital assets from a user and technology management perspective in estate planning, estate advisors, their supporting organizations, and online businesses should feel armed with the questions to ask and answers to provide when guiding individual clients through digital estate management, while offering insights into the future of the industry. Recognizing the value of further exploration of the topic, estate advisors will gain perspective on how to begin the digital journey within their professions, practices, and organizations. This book will expand an advisor's comfort with digital assets, providing a precursor into what will become a much bigger digital wave.

The intent of this book is to raise awareness on digital assets and the impact the internet and technology has on estate planning and financial and wealth management across the death care and estate industries. This book was written for a global audience of estate advisors, tech consultants, and any individual looking for a deeper understanding of the industry. It explores four avenues:

1. The context of where technology fits in a client's estate, an advisor's profession, and organizational practices.

2. The fundamental reasons why the digital topic is critical to advisors.
3. A deep dive into various digital assets within a client's portfolio, introducing an advisor to the technical management and user aspects of the topic. This section is the bulk of the book.
4. The book leaves the reader with a context of where digital assets sit in the broader digital transformation underway in the estate industry, and the impact this transformation is likely to have on individual businesses serving clients and their estate fiduciary and advisors.

Although the target audience of the book is estate advisors, the perspective is user-centric, guiding the advisor on a digital journey through the changing role of the fiduciary. This should illustrate to any advisor or organization the implication of a client's use of technology on not only estate planning and incapacity planning, but also estate administration. It is written in plain language and illustrated with everyday examples, establishing it as a perfect client gift from financial, legal, tax, insurance, technical, service provider, and gift planners.

As estate advisors, we know what can often be anxiety-fraught outcomes in situations when an individual dies without a will and an estate plan, or even when basic estate hygiene elements such as insurance policies and beneficiary designations are not addressed. These same risks apply to digital assets, but there are greater impacts and more barriers to remedies after death than for physical assets. Unless your client takes specific pre-planning actions for digital assets, their fiduciary will not be able to do much after the fact. If I could leave you with one fundamental digital asset planning tenet to share with your client, it is this: digital assets need documented estate plans. If your clients do not plan in advance to include their digital assets as part of their estate, these assets will likely be invisible, unavailable, or inaccessible for disbursement or transfer to beneficiaries.

The book also heightens awareness beyond the fundamentals

of digital assets to the broader discussion on the transformation of the death care and estate industry, prompted by the pandemic, resulting in virtual court proceedings, remote will-signing, electronic and digital signatures, electronic wills, and the front and back office transformation about to happen in every company, firm, and organization related to the estate industry. There will be other advisors who will write about the legal, tax, gift planning, insurance, and myriad of other estate planning and estate administration aspects of this digital assets topic as well as the digitization of the estate industry.

My first book, *Your Digital Undertaker: Exploring Death in the Digital Age in Canada*, was about digital assets in the context of an individual's or client's estate planning life cycle. This follow-up book, *Digital Executor®: Unraveling the New Path for Estate Planning*, is about digital assets in the context of the estate industry and the implications of the changing role of the fiduciary/executor. To understand the role of digital assets in the estate industry, we first need to understand technology and the changing role of the estate advisor.

Throughout this book, I'll refer to businesses, organizations, and tech entrepreneurs who provide technology, platforms, and services that allow consumers and businesses to interact online collectively as *service providers*. I'll refer to various professionals or practitioners involved fully or partly in estate planning, incapacity planning and/or estate administration, as *estate advisors*, which include legal advisors, tax advisors, insurance advisors, financial advisors, funeral and death care professionals, estate practitioners, estate planners, estate administrators, trustees, advisors to the fiduciary, agents to the fiduciary, technical advisors, gift planners, philanthropy advisors, and gift administrators.

Introduction

The Digital Age Is Here

How do we know that the advance care planning, end-of-life planning, death care, and funeral and estate industries are well on their way to being digitized, uberized, transformed, and innovated in ways we never expected? Because the digital headline hijacking has begun. The dotcom of the estate industry is here, because the pandemic has not only jump-started but also accelerated the digitization of the industry.

Jurisdiction-specific estate legislation and court processes have been evolving to leverage technology, but the pandemic has fast-tracked the global digitization conversation among advisors, clients, legislators, and the courts. A conversation that starts with the laws and processes allowing specific aspects of legal documents to be digitized is a thin edge of the digital wedge. Multifaceted digitization is expected from estate industry organizational processes that engage and support clients as well as from court processes and procedures. And watch this space for new entrants to the fray: tech entrepreneurs and service providers.

With the pandemic driving a renewed interest in technology and digitization, many articles of late have either hinted at, examined, or pecked at the matter of the future disruption anticipated by technology across multiple industries. If we step back and listen to the collective conversational hum of social media and the popping kernels of point-specific solutions, it's evident that tech incubators are attempting to address gaps in estate industry applications, from memorialization to business process solution refinement, through digitization.

Consider the pandemic paradigm as the technological transformative impetus to the legal and estate industries. No entity or organization will be immune to the effect that pervasive digitization will have on business processes and knowledge management hubs. Advisors, clients, tech entrepreneurs, and the broader industry are calling now as the time to embrace the digital agenda to improve services, innovate archaic processes, and perhaps even leapfrog the competition while improving client expectation management.

In 2017, when I was launching my tech management consultancy in estate planning, I wrote a framework paper about the digitization of the estate industry. As I am a process (industrial) engineer, the paper was complete with diagrams, flow charts, and explanations about the main business processes within the estate industry that would likely be affected and transformed by digitization.

I had hoped this model would help advisors identify where digital change or innovation was occurring in their estate business processes. But other than my esteemed colleagues in the Society of Trust and Estate Practitioners (STEP), a global society of estate professionals, Digital Assets Global Special Interest Group, (SIG) who were already involved in digital law reform with model laws such as electronic will legislation and money discussions in light of blockchain and cryptoassets, the interest among general estate advisors just wasn't there. So, for the last several years in the specialized space of digital assets in estate planning, I have felt like Bill Murray's character Phil in *Groundhog Day* trying to convince the estate and financial advisory audience that the digital tsunami is coming and advisors need to get ready. Now, well into the pandemic, the digital conversation has dramatically changed, evident from the questions I get from estate advisors and clients. The questions have shifted from what a digital asset is and why passwords are not the answer in estate planning to the future of electronic wills.

The digital pandemic shift was never more pronounced than when I presented to advisors at the Canadian Association of Gift Planners (CAGP) summer school event in July 2020. The presentation umpire pitched me a barrage of questions well beyond digital assets to include pure electronic assets from this highly engaged audience. This estate gift planning audience was keen on talking about electronic will legislation, the role that DIY online will apps play, client expectations in the digital paradigm, and the future of tech in the estate world—elements that go well beyond the conversation on a client's personal digital assets or how the internet has broken estate administration. The buzz surrounding and acceleration of the topic has been swirling since the onset of the pandemic.

Your clients may not consider their newfound digital existence through Zoom, ordering groceries, conducting financial transactions, or engaging with their physician virtually as the foundation for a digital estate, but all of these activities are tied to digital assets and must be considered in your clients' estate plans.

The pervasive use of the internet, the degree to which digital assets differ, and the variance in client wishes and preferences are as divergent as we've seen for physical assets and property rights. There is a shift in thinking required to deal with digital assets: if clients do not plan for their digital assets, likely the assets will be invisible, inaccessible, or nontransferable upon incapacity and/or death.

Given the significant sentimental and financial value digital assets could hold, a client's digital portfolio needs the same care and attention an advisor would provide when dealing with physical assets.

The purpose of this book is to raise the estate advisor's awareness of the impact that clients' digital lives and digital footprint have on their estate plan and on the estate industry. This is not a book about the scourge of COVID-19, particularly because we don't know how that story ends, but any topic in today's climate that touches on death and estate planning cannot be relevant without acknowledging the pandemic and the change in people's behavior.

Our clients' digital lives and digital footprint are an emerging area in the death care and estate planning community and this book deals with the five pillars of the framework to ready advisors for operating in the technology-driven world.

The foundational framework is as follows:

- Technology is the new player at your client's planning table.
- Death with a side of digital.
- Your money, your memory, your records: recognizing digital assets.
- Today's fiduciary is a digital fiduciary (e.g., executor, attorney, or estate trustee).
- The digital estate planning tsunami.

Technology Is the New Player at Your Client's Estate Planning Table

Believe it or not, technological advancement or evolutionary innovation doesn't occur randomly or by happenstance.

In consulting terms, there is a pattern to the lightning pace of change, and it boils down to two repeating cycles. Embracing the notion of change gives insight to the transformation happening in the death care and estate industries.

- In every industry, inventors or the early adopters introduce technology or innovative leaps as competitive advantages, giving one business an edge over another.
- Over time, technology redefines what are the competitive necessities, the minimum requirements customers expect in the marketplace.

An obvious example is the financial sector. Today you wouldn't dream of opening a new bank without online services or a mobile client app.

Two simple steps and the cycle repeats itself with the next iteration or invention. In today's tech environment, innovation or evolution is happening with blockchain, robotics, artificial intelligence, and quantum computing. The concepts of competitive advantage and competitive necessity have been table stakes in the Management Information Systems (MIS) research and literature, presented in journals such as the *Journal of Strategic Information Systems* and *MIS Quarterly*; however, I first read about these value chain and strategic information systems (IS) terms in one of Michael E. Porter's early books. This simple construct has stuck with me through many years of technical industry innovation life cycles.

Death With a Side of Digital

Every sector and industry have been transformed by our use of technology and the internet. Within the financial sector we have seen retail banking transformation, retirement planning transformation, the emergence of fintech along with the overall disruption of financial institutions.

In addition, Millennials, GenZ, and Coronials—a newly minted term for those born during the COVID-19 era—will have their own client expectations of the death care and estate industries in the coming years, including opinions on philanthropy and charity. They will ask questions such as—What about electronic wills? Can I put my will on the blockchain? Can I set up a social media trust as well as a pet trust? Why can't I manage my parent's estate administration through an app like I do for online banking? Or, why has my estate advisor not provided an online inventory tool to track my assets or an estate planning platform to house all my estate documents and requirements? And so here comes "estatetech."

Your Money, Your Memory, Your Records: Recognizing Digital Assets

Your clients have a new class of assets called digital assets, but this term is just not that user-friendly. A better way to refer to what jurisdictional laws define as *electronic records* is to think of digital assets *as memories, money, and records that are now in digital form instead of on paper.* You'll want to refer to your specific juris-diction for a formal definition. STEP defines digital assets as *items that have some of the same characteristics as do physical assets, such as financial or sentimental value.*

It might seem helpful to contrast digital assets to physical assets by making the case that physical assets are the things we can touch and see, such as real property and tangible personal items, whereas digital assets are intangible. But the matter can quickly get complicated considering many of the things we own are not physical at all but are extensions of choices we make, such as the debt we incur, the investments we make, or the work product of creativity resulting in intellectual property. The lines are further blurred when our access to physical assets might be managed through a digital account, making the point for how intertwined our physical assets rights might be with our digital footprint.

We don't have hundreds of years of legal precedents or expe-rience to guide us here given there is a multitude of applicable, different, and new jurisdictional laws on the topics of fiduciary access, privacy, property rights, and tax that are still years behind the wake of constantly evolving technology and the develop-ment of new types of digital asset classes. Further, many of these digital assets are constrained by service providers in their terms of service agreed to by clients. I'm referring to the reams of screens most of us, including your clients, scroll through before we blindly click the agree button. Deciphering provider terms of service alone will spawn a tremendous amount of work as every digital asset your client owns has different characteristics that need examina-tion and analysis to effectively provide estate planning guidance. We wouldn't dismiss a bank account with hundreds of dollars, so why should we dismiss our client's digital assets?

Although we can call digital assets a new asset class, they aren't really new. Digital assets emerged with the advent of the information age—a period we can all agree began in earnest with the rise of the world wide web or internet, over 30 years ago.

The way we communicate and engage socially has transformed

from physical letters to e-mail and social media—in other words, as a result of digital assets.

Long before the pandemic, digitization and automation critically impacted the traditional workplace:

- In the retail sector, many stores moved from traditional brick-and-mortar storefronts to online stores.
- The financial sector is well aware of the transformative impact of technology with online accounts and mobile apps.
- Supermarkets offer online ordering, airlines offer online ticket booking, ride sharing services are completely online for ordering, paying, and rating.

Technology and the pandemic have changed how services are delivered and new markets are reached.

Today's Fiduciary Is a Digital Fiduciary

Effectively, the age of the mailbox is all but gone.

Estate advisors who have considered digital assets only on their own are acknowledging the tip of the iceberg but may have overlooked the implications of the digital age to the fiduciary's role. Digital assets are certainly important, but there is another essential industry transformation issue at play. The fiduciary's role during estate administration has fundamentally changed as a result of the shift from a paper to a paperless society.

Even if you concentrate on estate planning, you have an obligation to recognize and inform your clients how technology has impacted the fiduciary's role in estate administration. It's not only prudent to advise a client of these changes, but down the road, it's reasonable to anticipate that beneficiaries will hold estate planners to account. Even if we set aside potential liability risks to the advisor and/or the fiduciary, consider that beneficiaries will likely take to social media to share unhappy experiences with organizations upon the death of the account holder, potentially leading to an entire generation seeking alternative service providers who address their need for transparency, speed, and efficiency during such an emotional and challenging time.

If you boil down the fiduciary's job, the elemental steps in their role are to follow the will or court order, retrieve or create an asset/property inventory, close down the testator's life by paying off the bills and taxes, and then disperse the remaining assets according to the will. What is absolutely central to their ability to perform their duties is captured in the proverbial estate inventory or estate binder, a listing or paper trail of the testator's assets and liabilities.

The paper-filled era gave the fiduciary a fighting chance with printed statements. With all of us online for everything, including managing our households and filing taxes, the fiduciary will likely be faced with a locked computer or device screen with potentially limited or no ability legally or otherwise to access. The fiduciary's job is thwarted right out of the gate with implications that could drive increased cost and effort in estate administration and in the worst case frustrate the testator's wishes if assets are never found.

The fundamental success of the fiduciary, after finding the signed physical will, depends on their ability to create a list or inventory of all the things the deceased person owned. Even a cursory look at the person's life, which the fiduciary is responsible for shutting down, will show how the digital age has further complicated the fiduciary's job.

The question remains: How does this digital transformation affect advisors serving clients as wealth and estate advisors?

For those advisors working in estate administration today, when dealing with older clients, they might see only the occasional e-mail account, social media account, or one household laptop, but this profile of usage and ownership is rapidly changing. Fortunately, the distressing cases of beneficiaries and fiduciaries needing to go to court to access a deceased person's e-mail or photos are still few and far between, but the question persists: How many are abandoning the digital legal cause or are completely unaware of a loved one's digital footprint after their incapacity and/or death?

The accepted stereotype of older clients, say, people over the age of 65, is that this age group is less tech-savvy and therefore would have a small or negligible digital footprint. But internet statistics paint a different picture. According to *Internet World Stats*:

- In North America, 90% of the population uses the internet and 76% are Facebook users.
- In Europe, 87% of the population uses the internet.
- Globally, 63% of the world's population uses the internet.

Pre-pandemic, we would have said that as information technology (IT) moved to the personal realm, the internet wasn't just a toy used for entertainment, it was part of our client's day-to-day lives, but the pandemic changed everything. If your client, as a result of the pandemic, is now using a video conferencing app, ordering groceries, conducting financial transactions online, connecting virtually with their family doctor, has taken up a hobby, started a small business or engages with others via social media to pass the time, they now have a digital estate.

The Digital Estate Planning Tsunami

Inclusion of tech management considerations in an estate plan is a new requirement as we see clients not planning for their digital assets, rendering them invisible, inaccessible, or nontransferable upon incapacity and/or death.

The basic planning tenet must be that digital assets are different than physical assets—yet they still require the same attention to detail, and perhaps more.

Estate planning of our digital lives includes providing tech instructions, documenting plans, and testing tech instructions and backup plans. This preparation is not dissimilar in many ways to IT planning in a business context with the transition, and business continuity and business succession planning now needing to be applied to our home IT. Included should be a review of the technical management plan with the fiduciary, incorporating a dry run.

Effective estate planning for digital assets requires concerted effort on behalf of the client while they are alive. Because a client's data privacy and security after death can be impacted by sloppy IT hygiene during life, a client who doesn't maintain their tech risks introduces threats to their privacy and data, potentially exposing them to identity theft and cybercrime not only while alive, but also upon incapacity, or to their estate after death.

The fiduciary will no longer be able to just show up after death and figure out a testator's digital life and digital estate, never mind finding all the physical property rights with the paper trail now having gone digital.

Estate planners should encourage clients to protect themselves online. The advisor's scope will likely expand to include recommendations for client adherence to tech best practices for digital device management, including strengthening secure access, operating system currency, backup execution, and referrals to technical advisors and service provider for best practices. Such advice is not that different from advice you might provide for physical assets and property rights, be that real estate, or art or other collectables that typically retain value only if they are looked after, protected, and maintained.

Project Management Applied:
Planning a Death Project in the Digital Age

The idea of getting your affairs in order can be uplifting, particularly if you consider who you are getting your affairs in order for—your loved ones and beneficiaries. The least stressful path for getting your affairs in order is to remove the emotion by planning and preparing just like you would for a home renovation project. But this time, the project is your death project.

Treating death like a project reduces the inherent emotional reaction to it being a sensitive and morbid subject. No one wants to die. Some of us think that if we ignore it, it won't happen. This thinking allures us with magic, but it's unrealistic.

Within the technology industry, project management is used to help organizations and clients achieve their business goals and technology objectives. Project management is applied to everything from launching new products and creating new software to creating new client solutions. Treating your individual death like a project, your death project, can help avoid magical thinking.

A project is about tackling something new, getting something specific done that likely produces a result, usually within a defined time period. A project normally has an agreed-upon scope that sets out its immediate goal. Projects involve coordinating people and resources and are not something you do regularly. Projects may be described as things that are temporary and unique.

When it comes to death, there are two unique projects involved: the testator's death project, which is getting the will and estate plan in order, and the fiduciary's death project, happening after death, which is the administration of the decedent's estate.

Estate Industry Digitization

It is my sincere wish that you, the reader, enjoy the pilgrimage into the converging worlds of tech and the estate industry as you build awareness of the estate industry's digital transformation journey. When you, as an advisor, engage early, you can ensure your clients are fully aware of how to maximize the value of all their assets—digital and physical—and the greater competitive advantage you will have in the industry. Because soon, it will be a competitive necessity.

Chapter One

Technology Is the New Player at the Estate Planning Table

How the Internet Broke Estate Planning

When the internet first appeared, it began as static web pages of content, simply a new channel of information businesses made available to clients. It wasn't long until businesses and IT companies recognized its commercial value and one industry after another began to transform with it now on an exponential growth curve. Social media is now part of daily life, and every other day we hear about another innovation, acquisition, or entrepreneurial company born from technological advancement.

We may eventually transition to a comfortable place as users do with any new innovation, but there is often disruption, or at least discomfort, at the outset. Today is no different with the polarization in opinion on the emergent blockchain technology, a decentralized token ledger of unregulated cryptocurrencies in this evolutionary mix. But undoubtedly blockchain too will change and adapt to company needs and consumer marketplace demands.

We know the digital world has changed just about every sector, our workplace, and our personal lives, but do we really understand how it has affected our clients' estates plans and the estate industry? It boils down to understanding four digital phenomena born of the internet age:

- Individuals have a digital estate in addition to a physical one.
- Physical and digital estates are intertwined.
- Estate advisors must stay current as jurisdictional legislation and case law evolve.
- Deeper conversations are required with clients on the role of their fiduciaries.

Clients Have a Digital Estate and a Physical One

The estate industry calls these new assets *digital assets*. We are the first generation of estate advisors dealing with clients who have wishes about passing along their digital estates. Digital assets, in their simplest form, are electronic records. The most common and recognizable digital assets are online accounts, including e-mail, social media, loyalty points, photos, and cloud storage repositories.

Although unregulated cryptocurrencies were invented in 2009, they didn't catch mainstream attention until 2017. Even so, 10 years ago, the idea that a client's digital footprint, e-mail, or social media accounts had any inherent estate planning value might have seemed absurd. This is no longer the case. Clients of all ages have strong preferences for what happens with their online lives after death, and these wishes and preferences deserve the same care and handling as their physical assets. Also demanding consideration are digital assets of sentimental or emotional value such as digital photos, genealogy records, or family histories, as they are likely no longer in paper format.

Digital assets can have financial value when you consider web domains, gaming tokens, ad-and-click revenue, the value of social media influencer accounts, and the fact that the gig economy is underpinned by apps and online platforms. Beyond the client's wishes and preferences regarding these assets upon incapacity or death, there could also be tax liability requiring consideration during estate planning.

This implies that estate advisors and organizations supporting the estate industry need to be comfortable asking a client about their digital lives. Digging under the covers of significant digital assets to advise clients on how to create specific estate plans for these assets and adding directives to wills and other documents will become the norm in the estate planning process.

Most online accounts and digital assets are governed by providers' terms of service contracts. With no consistency among digital custodians, you'll have to investigate these agreements individually to understand if your client is even able to transfer these assets. If technical management aspects of the transfer need to be pre-planned and documented, you'll have to consider service provider guidance or suggest a client get further technical advice.

Unregulated cryptocurrencies, future cryptoassets, or other blockchains bring their own unique characteristics. For today's currently unregulated cryptocurrencies, clients need estate plans that detail technical management instructions for fiduciary access and transfer instructions. Given the nature of blockchains, there isn't a central authority or password reset for cryptocurrencies.

Physical and Digital Estates Are Intertwined

A further conundrum is created when physical property rights intertwine with the digital world. If your client is a book author, you may be familiar with intellectual property rights and royalties, and have considered those elements in estate planning, but did you ask where the client keeps all the information supporting the copyright and copies of draft works and completed manuscripts? What if, in the digital age, your client now saves all this information and work in their e-mail account, cloud drive, or encrypted drive?

These questions should identify what additional and specific estate plans need to be documented for the technical management and practical aspects of a client's digital assets. Questions such as, Will the storage source be accessible to the fiduciary to fulfill the directives in the will or estate plan? Is there a backup copy stored safely, such as in a safety deposit box or held securely with a custodian? The client's intentions could be completely frustrated, because you or the client don't take the conversation one step further into the client's use of technology in managing those traditional property rights.

Stay Current as Jurisdictional Legislation and Case Law Evolves

Your client's estate administration could be fraught with landmines in the digital age as there are many jurisdiction-specific laws and rules for dealing with what might appear to be simple digital assets. And the world is still grappling with unregulated cryptocurrencies and what is and isn't considered property and their associated rights.

On the matter of fiduciary access laws, for example, many estate advisors in the United States know most states have adopted fiduciary access laws regarding digital assets. However, there are significant implications to these laws that most clients will not be familiar with. Most clients likely assume their appointed fiduciary will be allowed access to anything the deceased person had access to; even without a will, most assume the court-appointed fiduciary will have the same rights.

Not so with the US *Revised Uniform Fiduciary Access to Digital Assets Act* (RUFADAA). Under RUFADAA, the fiduciary has some rights to access specific types of digital assets, but anything related to communication such as e-mail, text messages, and social media accounts must be pre-planned by the client (testator, will-maker) while they are living. More clearly, this means the law does not allow the fiduciary to deal with our digital lives unless such directives were documented in a will or legally recognized directive. In the absence of such a directive, the fiduciary will likely be required to engage in protracted and expensive court processes against the service provider for access to the digital asset if certain circumstances are met, but that still does not guarantee access will be achieved.

Estate advisors will have to first understand their own jurisdiction-specific laws with respect to accessing digital assets when explaining this risk to clients and encourage them to update their will and estate plans. Second, multiple jurisdictional laws may be involved, depending on how the client uses technology, what it is called, where they live, and where the technology provider is based, which will also need to be addressed.

Conversations With Clients on the Role of the Fiduciary

Traditional estate planning conversations about the fiduciary focus on the selection process: identifying the right person with the skills, time, and ability to manage the estate administration process. But in the digital age, such traditional estate planning conversations are not enough.

Your client's online footprint is the essence of a modern home office. Most people interact with their financial institutions online, transmit all of their correspondence electronically, and conduct all of their personal transactions from paying bills to booking travel and appointments online.

The fiduciary's success completely depends on finding, inventorying, and securing the assets and property rights of the deceased. Corporate/professional fiduciaries, trust companies, and fiduciary checklists have long relied on traditional mailbox and paper statements to help the fiduciary confirm or, in the worst case, reverse engineer the testator's life to locate property and assets.

Not having access to a client's asset inventory might mean the fiduciary is scrambling to get access to a client's e-mail. Without pre-planning or a jurisdiction-specific court order, the fiduciary won't have access to the digital trail of the client's assets, bills, liabilities, and contacts. This means the fiduciary's job just got stymied, which will impact and frustrate the testator's intentions, potentially leaving the beneficiaries with less than what they expected. The issue is that clients' online accounts are virtual with an invisible trail. Our clients stand to lose not only their digital assets but also the trail to their physical assets if the fiduciary is denied access.

Very few technology providers have pre-planning options. Facebook's Legacy Contact and Google's Inactive Account

Manager are two examples where the account owner can identify and give pre-planned access to an individual under specific conditions. The key is that these actions must be taken in advance.

I hope that as consumers become aware of jurisdiction-specific laws covering access and the limitations imposed by service providers, they will demand more pre-planning options to deal with the entanglement of their physical lives with their ever-growing digital lives.

Any estate advisor would be well advised to spend more time pre-planning their clients'digital assets and reminding them of the value of an estate binder, including listings of their physical and digital assets. Paper trails still have value in the digital age, but there will be continued demand for products and services as consumer awareness and grows.

Stepping up the risk assessment associated with the fiduciary role and ferreting out the risks and mitigations that clients hadn't considered regarding the fiduciary's ability to find, access, and transfer assets as per their wishes should be part of the pre-planning process.

What can estate advisors do to raise their level of awareness? Consider these starting points:

- **Develop an understanding of the impact the digital age is having on the estate industry:** Engage with your professional associations, your estate planning organizations, and within your own organizations to determine if there is special guidance, special interest groups, or communities of interest to share information about digital assets within your jurisdiction. As the laws evolve and catch up, your firms and associations are likely developing processes, practices, and tools to deal with digital assets and the transformative impact that technology will have on not only estate processes but also organizational engagement with clients.

    ○ For example, consider the STEP SIG. Currently, any global advisor can join (one need not be a STEP member) and is currently no charge. STEP provides jurisdiction-specific guidance and checklists, such as the *Inventory for Digital Assets and Digital Devices*, for use with clients.

- **Consider forming an organizational program, policy team, forum, or special project on digital assets within your profession and/or organization:** Every estate-related profession and organization will need to create or update policies, practices, tools, and procedures to deal with a client's digital assets in estate planning, incapacity planning, and estate administration.

  ○ For example, if you recommend your client create an inventory for their assets and property rights, this inventory will need to be updated to address digital assets.

- **Building confidence with the digital assets topic in your estate practice:** In 2013, the American Bar Association updated sections of its professional responsibility standards and set expectations for its lawyers "to better deal with technology and its effects on lawyers' practices." Within the estate specialty, such advice means familiarization with the digital asset implications of estate planning, incapacity planning, and estate administration. Your professional development could include digging into the terms of service of your clients' digital assets, educating yourself on technology use, and becoming more aware of privacy and cybersecurity practices.

  ○ For example, one initiative started by three US-based lawyers, Jennifer Zegel, Ross Bruch, and Justin Brown, is the *Digital Planning Podcast* (DPP). This podcast hosts interview guests from many different industries to cover relevant and timely topics about the digitization of the estate industry and digital assets regarding estate planning, business planning, and estate administration.

The amount of lost or inaccessible assets will grow and estate administration will become more challenging with the proliferation of digital assets in our clients' portfolios. Clients and their families (as beneficiaries) will be distressed if their assets are lost. They will ask you why you didn't advise them to get a will, create an asset inventory, sort out their digital lives, and prepare the fiduciary. The digital age has changed everything. Fundamentally, how families communicate is part of this change.

Clients will expect an increased level of knowledge from their estate advisors on how to deal with this new asset class, service providers, and evolving jurisdictional laws. The more you can do to ensure your clients are fully aware of how to maximize the value of ALL their assets—regular, unique, and digital, the greater value you will have with clients in this growing and evolving field.

The Digital Paradigm Shift

There are three factors that demand estate advisors gain a better understanding of their clients' digital assets and the underlying technology in order to provide informed advice.

- The pervasiveness of the client's use of the internet.
- The degree to which digital assets differ.
- Client wishes for digital assets are as varied as they are for physical assets.

The internet, and our clients' use of technology, was already changing the death care and estate industries long before the pandemic. The social distancing demanded by COVID-19 has accelerated our clients' engagement with the digital world, reigniting the topic of digital asset management, which will demand a transformation in estate planning.

Dealing with a client's digital assets and their all-encompassing digital estates, including their digital footprint and wishes for their digital legacy, is not as simple as drafting a tidy digital assets blanket clause in their will. This is such an important topic that we're all going to have to roll up our sleeves to get a better understanding of the problem and how to address it.

The digital topic needs the same care and attention an advisor would provide when dealing with physical assets and property rights given the significant sentimental and financial value digital assets may hold. Unquantified client requirements will have a widespread impact on the estate industry, including the development of client estate plans, creating stress on estate planning and administrative policies and practices.

Historically, the estate industry often waits for jurisdictional law in the form of legislation and case law before updating estate policies and practices. Estate advisors may be well versed in the practical elements related to property rights, but they should also understand the technical aspects of digital assets; that is, the practical elements of the underlying technology, such as the constraints of provider terms of service and the need for broader provider tech management pre-planning options. It's imperative that, while waiting for the application of jurisdictional law, you raise your knowledge of the technology management aspects of digital assets and begin updating your processes and practices.

The estate management requirements of our clients' growing portfolio of digital assets are an emerging area for the estate industry and estate advisors. To incorporate digital assets into estate planning, we will examine how the estate industry could approach a client's digital estate from a business enterprise perspective.

When Stars Align: Working with IT
to Tackle Digital Estate Planning

Given the estate industry is on the cusp of dealing with digital estate management, we can look to academia for guidance and leverage a model developed in the early days of IT when business was grappling with how to leverage IT for their business processes. The information technology alignment model called *A Model of Factors That Influence the Social Dimension of Alignment*, first introduced by Dr. Blaize Horner Reich and Dr. Izak Benbasat, has stood the test of time and can serve as a valuable framework. I had the privilege of working with Dr. Reich and Dr. Benbasat in applying this IT Alignment Model to the Canadian Armed Forces

27

in examining the early stages of IT adoption to provide recommendations on effectively leveraging and integrating IT in the military business processes.

A Shift in Estate Thinking

This IT Alignment Model is based on the premise that to achieve business or organizational outcomes, IT objectives should be aligned with business objectives to do the following:

- Drive the business forward
- Meet client expectations
- Leapfrog the competition

Recognizing that IT and business didn't have a long history of working well together enabled the development of this framework to coach and guide leaders on how to engage.

In many ways, this is an ideal model to apply to the estate industry for dealing with technology as the emergent player at the table and the client's digital asset portfolio. For the first time in history, all estate advisors will need to deal with a client's individual digital estate, whereas up until now, technology may have only been a factor in the exceptional or ad hoc estate situation, or part of a company's business succession planning. When looking at a client's digital footprint, their use of the internet has also created a digital barrier in estate administration, if you consider technology solely from the perspective of how paperless our clients' home offices are and the resulting impact on the fiduciary's role.

How Does the IT Alignment Model Work?

The model is brilliant in its simplicity. In order for IT to be aligned to the business to provide the best results, there are identifiable factors that affect the social dimension of alignment, namely:

- Shared domain of knowledge
- Success in IT implementation
- Communication and connections between the business and IT planning

Shared domain of knowledge is simply the idea that business needs to learn enough about IT, and IT needs to learn enough about business so that a common understanding can lead to the best outcomes. If nothing else, shared domain of knowledge makes communication and planning easier.

Success in IT implementation is the idea that past success can foster future success. The idea is that if the business has successfully worked with IT in the past, it is more likely to communicate or plan with IT in the future.

Communication and planning affect alignment directly. Intuitively, this should make sense because what project or process involving technology has worked without communication and planning? Probably none. In most cases, if something isn't planned, it's unlikely to happen, or it can have unintended consequences—not unlike in the estate world when a client dies intestate (without a will and/or estate plan). And with any project or endeavor to achieve the business goal, the scope needs to be controlled, the risks and issues managed, making communication paramount to keep expectations aligned.

Factors That Influence the Social Dimension of Alignment as Applied to Estate Planning and Estate Administration

Visualize the following: If alignment between estate advisors and IT is the ultimate outcome for success in dealing with a client's digital assets, then consider the antecedents required. First is the notion of a shared domain of knowledge pertaining to a client's digital assets. For example, do estate advisors understand the implications of provider terms of service and tech pre-planning options, and do tech advisors appreciate the implications of their tech practices as they relate to the estate industry and estate/trustee law?

The second is the desired success in implementation of the management of digital assets wherein estate advisors have engaged and worked successfully with IT service providers.

These antecedents drive the current practices, and the current practices influence alignment. The first interlock dependency in current practices relates to communication between the estate industry and the tech industry; the second are the connections between estate and IT planning.

Applying the Reich and Benbasat (2000) Model of Factors That Influence the Social Dimension of Alignment to the Estate Industry in Dealing With Digital Assets in Estate Planning

In an estate planning example, if you and a colleague have worked together on a client estate file with past success, you are both likely to want to work together again. This behavior is reasonably pervasive and encouraged in the estate industry when you consider the multi-disciplinary elements of a client's estate plan. For example, a legal advisor might refer a client to a specific tax advisor, or vice versa. Similarly, if you are uncomfortable with a topic or haven't worked with a colleague in a specific area, you might be less likely to engage with them.

How Does the Model Help the Estate Industry?

Let's consider the alignment of a client's use of technology and the estate industry. The shared domain of knowledge is one of the two basic building blocks in the model. In the digital context, this means that estate advisors need to be comfortable with the user aspects of digital assets and their underlying technology, and service providers need to be comfortable with the business processes and laws that apply to the estate industry.

There are several ways to accomplish this, including reading, researching, technical learning, working on a case involving a digital asset, or attending a conference. The learning curve might be flattened by your use of technology at work and home, creating a deeper comfort zone.

The Contextual Framework

Noting context orients us to what kind of digitization we're talking about. With that grounding, an estate advisor can use context as a basis for their own transformation roadmap. In some respects, we are in a race to define this framework across the profession. Many variations of labels will surface, but eventually language will standardize. Simply put, if you can't name it or point to it, you can't replace it, improve it, or innovate it.

Consulting firms create a library of component business models for every industry, sector, and subspecialty. This labeling informs discovery and serves as the basis for benchmarking when improving business processes by adding or replacing IT solutions.

We know that a picture is worth a thousand words. A simple diagram, picture, framework, or infographic that gives context to the digital transformation the estate industry can serve as a starting point in understanding the disruption. Such visual representations can further serve to provide a roadmap while navigating who's who, and what's what, in the landscape of the ever-evolving estate industry.

There is no single way to represent the business processes of the estate world. Any visual representation that makes sense for our clients or our industry will do. Since there is no correct way to draw the estate industry contextual diagram, I use a variety of techniques to illustrate the major business processes of the industry, recognizing they are integrated and overlapping. As an example, here is a simple list of macro business processes I see for the estate industry:

- Client digital assets as a new asset class
- Client-facing front-office processes
- Organization back-office processes
- Jurisdictional estate law and legislation
- Jurisdictional or procedural court estate processes
- Other digitization affecting the estate industry
- Stakeholder engagement with service providers, online businesses, and the tech industry

These representations illustrate a framework while acknowledging that disruption of one element could upset the entire apple cart. Other dimensions such as tax, legal, philanthropy, gift planning, insurance, financial management, and technical management need be layered into the framework.

- **Client digital assets as a new asset class:** This is not so much a business process as a macro component for the framework, but the discussion needs to start here.

    Even if there is a will, the deceased can't ask from the grave why you didn't have them create an asset inventory, or discuss the necessity of sorting out their digital lives, or the impact the digital age has had on their estates, but dissatisfied beneficiaries and fiduciaries can.

    Prior to the pandemic, I could easily list the tech companies with digital inventory solutions to manage digital assets. In the *STEP Journal* article "Bolster Your Digital Armoury" these estate tools are called *digital vaults*. Since the pandemic, I've lost track of the explosion of tech entrepreneurs who are building or have built applications to address not only an individual's personal digital assets inventory but also inventories for all of an individual's physical property rights and digital assets.

- **Client-facing front-office processes:** This aspect of the framework includes policies, practices, and tools to first, meet client rights under jurisdictional law, and second, deal with client engagement in estate planning, incapacity planning, and administration. Social media and the digital age are changing how clients and their families communicate with estate advisors and professionals such as financial planners. The front office is where we'll see estate platforms or tools for client engagement.

    We know that e-mail is an insecure means of communication and that the financial and insurance sectors have already moved to secure platforms for client relationship management, including adopting tools such as signature capture. Clients will expect similar interfaces within the estate industry.

We'll also need to educate our clients on their use of digital assets and the estate industry transformation. Raising client awareness on how their digital lives affect their estates and digital assets delves into client personal computing habits, including cybersecurity.

- **Organization back-office processes:** Day-to-day operations include accounting systems, administration, and IT management—all non-public-facing processes that keep the firm running, compliant, and aligned to client expectations. I expect businesses and professional associations to develop their own cross-disciplinary teams to drive the digital transformation agenda, allowing members to share learnings from estate administration into estate planning and vice versa—needed practices to assist in the adaptation into the digital age.

- **Jurisdictional estate law and legislation:** This contextual element includes current and future (proposed model) substantive and procedural rule of law, fiduciary rules, estate and inheritance laws, complex laws including cross-border law, conflict of law, and future laws dealing with estate planning and administration. This component also includes guidelines, procedures, and codes of ethics of professional associations and regulatory bodies that address estate planning, incapacity planning, and estate administration.

The adoption of electronic wills is a tremendous paradigm shift when historically wills have been paper based, signed, and validated with wet signatures, and here we are transitioning this complex directive to a digital format.

An important paper on the global state of the nation on electronic will legislation is "Technology and Wills: The Dawn of a New Era (COVID-19 Special Edition)," published by STEP. There is no such thing as a digital will per se, but jurisdictionally based electronic will legislation is emerging. The author of the paper, Kimberley Martin, also covers the distinction between digital and electronic signatures. I highly recommend reading this paper.

If we consider the legislative impact of electronic wills as a precursor to the broader discussion of estate planning, and if a will is the basic building block of an estate plan, then all the processes up to its creation and use during estate administration are implicated in the new digital equation. But it doesn't stop there. Through digitization, we'll be able to solve other cost and process problems that exist in a paper-based system. Electronic will registries and repositories for every type of instrument in an estate plan outside a will would be possible.

Other jurisdiction-specific legislation will change to address our digital lives both in life and death, such as post-mortem privacy. Expect to see articles and books on every type of estate-related legislation to be affected by technology. This is just the beginning.

- **Jurisdictional or procedural court estate processes:** If court-based rules allow for online probate submissions, estate planning professionals will need to think about how to collect client data for secure, timely, and integrated digital submissions. Is your firm enabled for online client submissions? But the more disruptive question is, Why does the client need the legal advisor or middleman if the court processes are automated?

- **Other digitization affecting the estate industry:** It's fair to say that when the financial industry sneezes, the estate industry gets a cold as a result of the overlapping business processes between these two worlds. Taxes are taxes, but there are subtle and substantive differences between those applicable to the living and those applicable to estates. Estate taxation, after all, is a professional specialization. In light of blockchain, questions on money, cryptoassets, and jurisdictional central banks considering blockchain for fiat currencies all impact the estate planning industry.

- **Stakeholder engagement with service providers, online businesses, and the tech industry:** A list of business processes wouldn't normally include a list of roles. We know that the estate industry has a number of advisory roles, including tax, legal, gift planning, insurance, and financial planning, among others. Given the dramatic impact that technology is about to have on the estate industry, it is worth calling out that the estate industry now includes a new role: technical advisor.

  We know stakeholder engagement is fundamental to success in any project, program, or campaign, outlined in the estate business–tech alignment model mentioned earlier in this chapter.

  Some of the key stakeholders in the digital assets client discussion are the service providers who provide products, offerings, platforms, and services to your clients, professions, and respective organizations. Estate advisors may have experience contacting a financial institution and dealing with their staff to transfer a bank account. In this new digital paradigm, estate advisors will need to be comfortable engaging with service providers and tech companies who now hold their clients' digital assets. The estate industry, estate organizations, and individual estate advisors will need to foster a relationship with tech companies. Such relationships could extend to any business that holds client information, such as a business that has a loyalty or travel rewards program.

  I'm so passionate on the subject of service providers as stakeholders in the estate industry conversation that I moderated a panel for STEP's SIG Spotlight Week 2020 titled Digital Assets in Estate Planning: Understanding the Technology/ Service Provider Viewpoint. The panel aimed to demonstrate the kind of regular conversations the estate industry and the tech industry need to have to best serve clients and end users. The forum was a resounding success, due in no small part to the guests who have been involved on the frontlines of digital assets research and delivery:

- David Michels, from Queen Mary University of London (UK), shared the "State of the Nation" on service provider terms of service when dealing with incapacity and/or death.
- Dr. Edina Harbinja, from Aston University (UK), shared her work and perspectives on post-mortem privacy. This is a complicated area because we may have post-mortem wishes about our data that could conflict with currently available options for access from service providers, but could also be different from the wishes of beneficiaries and executors who need information to do their job.
- A policy stakeholder engagement manager at Facebook talked about how Facebook approaches stakeholder engagement, taking us into the backroom on how teams are organized to deal with memorialization and Legacy Contact functions.
- Dr. Jed Brubaker, from the Identity Lab, is part of the Information Science department at the University of Colorado (US). Brubaker was involved as a consultant in the early days of the development of Facebook's Legacy Contact. Brubaker indicates his recent funding from The National Science Foundation for the Digital Hospice–identity lab project "will provide people with guidance on how to include technology in their end-of-life plans while also creating best-practices for technologists on how to design systems that support and honor those plans."

Each of these individuals provided tremendous value with their differing perspectives on policy, law, human-centric design, and tech.

Stay Informed: Consider Which Approach Suits You

Leigh Sagar, STEP Digital Assets SIG Committee chair and author of *The Digital Estate*, rolled up his sleeves on digital assets by diving into how computers and technology work through self-study, and then further delved into cryptocurrencies by attending tech meetups and connecting with other crypto enthusiasts. For the average estate advisor, this immersion might not be feasible.

On a practical level, you can start by asking your client about their top three digital assets and understanding how the applications work from a user perspective, determining if there are pre-planning options and inquiring about the provider's terms of service.

This exercise isn't about becoming a tech expert or advisor; it's about learning enough to properly advise a client and to recognize when to refer them to a technical expert as you would for any other estate specialty, such as tax, insurance, gift planning, or trust administration.

A corollary to how the estate industry advises the handling of client digital assets is how the tech industry supports the estate industry in preparing advisors to plan for the handling of a client's digital assets upon death. To improve its knowledge of the estate industry, the tech industry will need to understand the estate business.

As a career IT management practitioner entering the estate industry, I started by taking the STEP Diploma program to raise my understanding of estate processes and terminology to augment my practical experience. When I am approached by tech entrepreneurs and service providers in the estate space who are looking to learn about estate planning and estate administration of digital assets, I ask them about their knowledge of the estate industry. What is their firm's estate knowledge base? Do they have estate advisors on their staff? Do they have access to qualified estate advisors knowledgeable about laws in their jurisdiction? Do they have board representation from the estate industry, and are they engaged in estate industry forums and communities focused on raising knowledge in this space?

Five Considerations for Digitization:
Building Awareness Within an Estate Organization

Based on the premise that the tech and estate industries need to work together, and considering the framework shared earlier in this chapter, we can identify five areas that merit research and investigation within your respective organizations to acquire digital readiness beyond digital assets:

1. Establish a relationship with the tech industry and service providers: Key stakeholders in the digital transformation discussion are the service providers—those who provide products, offerings, platforms, and services to the estate industry. Estate business–tech alignment is required, and as estate advisors, you should expect tech to learn about the estate industry, and similarly advisors should learn about tech.

2. Develop a contextual framework for estate industry business processes: If nothing else, we'll need a taxonomy or industry standard framework with common language capturing the macro, micro, and nano business processes of our industry. In the consulting world, the broader context is captured as generic business processes, sometimes called component business models. The purpose of a component business model is to provide a framework to set context and aid communication on a topic, and I shared some examples earlier.

3. Prepare your organization's digital transformation plan. In your estate organization, you will need to document where you're going with a digital transformation roadmap that adapts to marketplace change. It's worth asking, what does digital transformation mean to your industry in general and to your organization specifically? Simplistically, digital transformation is applying technology or innovation to automate, integrate, or transform a business process to meet client needs, remain competitive, or overtake the competition. There is a wealth of knowledge in the public domain on business transformation and the supporting methodologies for implementation, so I won't summarize here, but expect to see new books for the estate industry on digital transformation.

4. Identify go-to resources for help. The engineering profession and use of the title "engineer" is regulated in some parts of the world—the practice of consulting and software development is not. As such, it's no surprise that cybersecurity issues are on the rise and consumers are left devastated by free platforms and data exploitation. Anyone can code and call themselves a consultant, and it's no wonder IT projects fail at the rate they do when inexperienced service providers attempt to execute. The estate industry is not that different. Buyer beware. Engage reputable, experienced, and recognized expertise. Check references, get referrals from trusted sources, and leverage skilled resources to manage milestones and progress, expectations and delivery. IT project management is the cornerstone of successful business technology projects. Start small, pilot, test, test again, document, train, then train again, and consider that every line of code could cost thousands of dollars to maintain over the life cycle of the application. Intuitively, the technical aspects of a digital transformation project need management, but that is only half the battle. Governance and change management at the board and executive level is required along with organizational, employee, and client engagement for successful implementation.

5. Get comfortable with technology regardless of estate profession. With any digital transformation plan comes the need for a more robust IT environment. If you do nothing but count the days to retirement or hope that digitization won't affect your practice, at minimum you need to develop IT policies and procedures that keep pace with privacy laws and client confidentiality laws that meet today's cybersecure requirements. We know that weak systems are targeted, and clients can no longer be expected to share personal information via e-mail. They will expect secure platforms and client management systems that aid decision-making and communication for themselves, and their beneficiaries and fiduciaries. Implementing any technology-based process requires change, and a surefire way to failure is neglecting internal and client training.

Case in Point: Client Management– Digital Asset Planning Guidance

Just as we've learned about physical assets, testators (will-makers) will have to pre-plan their digital assets if they want their wishes and preferences to be honored after death. To do so, they will continue to look to traditional estate advisors, but the conversation must expand to cover their digital assets.

The digital age is also marshaling the need for tighter integration between estate planning and estate administration due to the added complexities of digital assets. It's no longer as simple as letting the fiduciary figure it out. The estate advisor and their testator client must spend time assessing risks, educating the fiduciary, and leaving more detailed guidance and instructions beyond the will on how to deal with their digital footprint.

This work applies to every element of the estate administration process. Our collective knowledge about technology in the digital age needs a rethink for advisors to properly advise clients, and the information technology alignment model as applied to the estate industry shared earlier can provide a conceptional framework to better serve client needs.

With all innovation, including technology, comes tremendous opportunity. If we embrace change, we can leverage it for the benefit of our firms, our clients, and ourselves. As estate advisors, we have a unique opportunity to delve into digital estate planning at its inception and provide leadership to our peers and clients in navigating this new territory.

With emergent #estatetech and innovative thinking applied to every aspect of the estate planning process, from will creation to the transfer of our digital assets, we can expect disruption of the death care and the estate industry.

Financial institutions, trust companies, and financial and wealth management firms—fintech will not be isolated from the digital transformation revolution in estate administration. I would argue just the opposite.

Digital transformation in estate planning and administration will be driven by the broader financial industry as a result of the next generation of fiduciaries knocking on their doors. Our being on the cusp of the largest intergenerational wealth transfer in history implies that the volume of fiduciaries will increase, and this tech-savvy generation will expect technology readiness to access, transfer, or manage accounts.

Lacking traditional paper trails, fiduciaries determined to identify accounts and assets won't stop at one or two institutions known to be associated with the testator. Frustrated fiduciaries will turn to multiple financial institutions and technology service providers to determine if the testator had accounts at these institutions or with these providers.

Settling an estate is already a costly, time-consuming process and likely still a paper-intensive experience for any institution—even when the fiduciary knows what assets they are trying to access, transfer, or manage. The complexity mounts if the fiduciary doesn't know what accounts might exist.

This increased volume will drive the financial industry to automate, streamline, and develop new processes and solutions, as it recognizes the business imperative for cost effectiveness, market presence, and reputational authority.

Nor will the frustrated fiduciaries looking for information be quiet. They will take to social media to express their displeasure.

As a further example, the philanthropy sector has been affected by the digital age with crowdfunding.

Most important is the added value and leadership that we as individual advisors and members of the estate community must bring to our organization and community as the industry digitizes, noting the importance of the following:

- Building relationships with the tech industry and service providers.
- Understanding the contextual framework for estate industry business processes.
- Becoming familiar with your organization's digital transformation plan.
- Finding a set of go-to resources for help when playing in the digital transformation sandbox.
- Developing a level of comfort with technology regardless of profession.

Chapter Two
Death With a Side of Digital

The Digital Journey

Digitization as Table Stakes

Regardless of what the paradigm is called, the pandemic became the impetus for digital transformation in the estate industry. Estate advisors shouldn't underestimate the speed at which what was once a competitive advantage becomes a competitive necessity. If we insert the estate industry's digitization into the financial sector's transformation, consider the shifts in focus from retail banking to mobile banking, investment banking, then retirement banking, and now what I call *integrated estate banking*, or *estate banking* for short. The next generation will leap from "fintech" to "estatetech," from banking and investment platforms to various types of digital estate platforms, cross generational life planning platforms, integrated estate planning/administration platforms, and estate platform economy/ecosystems.

With any new bandwagon, we seek opportunities to get an edge. One of my favorite terms these days is *digital headline hijacking*, which is an oversimplistic phrase to describe articles with the word *digital* slapped to the front of the headline. In all fairness, we all strive to align client needs to the topic of the day to raise awareness of products, services, or offerings—also known as jumping on the bandwagon.

As a professional engineer, I've become increasingly troubled by the lack of definitions, inconsistent terminology, and the void of explanations setting the context when the term digital appears at the front end of every estate industry process.

We have all attended more webinars during 2020 than we thought possible, and one striking observation from estate industry conferences and legal industry forums is the lack of context, roadmap, or explanation when technological innovation is applied to create #estatetech or #digitalestate. I am often left with lingering questions. Is the technical thingamajig solving a little mess? Is it offering a new solution to a long-standing, medium-sized industry problem? Or is it a transformative solution to an integrated industry conundrum?

The excitement from clients who engage with tech and from the tech entrepreneurs plugging their digital wares is absolute, but frequently neither the business significance nor process being affected is stated in plain terms. Never mind the analysis on whether the solution is appropriate for other players in the same situation, if it would scale, integrate within the firm, connect outside the firm, transform the client experience, reduce cost, improve productivity, or meet stakeholder, shareholder, or business objectives. Without a framework, there are no benchmarks.

I've often been left wondering whether these companies or innovations will be here in a year or if they will die on the vine or be gobbled up by angel investors who really get where they fit in the integrated business spectrum. Perhaps the bigger question is whether big business or big tech will realize the estate industry paradigm shift and get on the bandwagon too.

Changing the Conversation in the Digital Age

We live in the digital era, where technology has transformed how we communicate and engage socially—even how we die. In any given year, more people are killed in accidents while taking selfies than from shark attacks. The term *selfie*, representative of the social media age, has even made it into the dictionary. Almost all of us have digital lives, even if these include just a subscription to the online edition of your favorite newspaper or magazine, or keeping up with friends via social media. And if you keep photos on your smartphone or save points on your loyalty card, you own digital assets. We are only beginning to realize the potential of technological innovations such as autonomous driving, block-chain, virtual reality, augmented reality, robotics, drones, artificial intelligence, and quantum computing, and are still coming to terms with the impact those inventions might have on our lives.

I used to think that the worst thing someone could do was leave a vast collection of possessions in their home, basement, attic, crawl space, or garage for their poor fiduciary to dispose of. I have experienced phone calls asking for help in clearing out a house or an apartment, and spent endless days separating the recyclables from the keepsakes. However, accumulating a large amount of stuff is not, from an estate planning perspective, the worst thing you can do. (Unless, of course, it's a major fire hazard. Then maybe it is.)

When you have gone to the great beyond, the easiest thing that the fiduciary may do—compared to filing probate, preparing taxes, managing beneficiaries, and navigating the instructions in your will and the law—is sort through the deceased person's physical pos-sessions. All that's involved is pulling together some help, locating the items mentioned in the will, then sorting and tossing out or donating what no one wants. There may even be a sense of satis-faction in getting it done. With the proliferation of companies in the junk trade and the emerging death cleaning businesses, it will be reasonably easy for the fiduciary to hire help or order one of those oversized commercial-grade steel garbage bins to be delivered to the front of the home.

Not to be flippant, but there are two opinions on how to deal with the mass of personal possessions. One side holds that the testator should get their house in order now by passing things along and reducing clutter. This is no different than what one might do if they wanted to downsize their home or if they decided to move. The thinking is that it is good for the testator, and their fiduciary, beneficiaries, and survivors. The opposing view is that sorting through a deceased person's treasures helps survivors get closure—that it's cathartic to revisit the past and reflect upon the deceased's life. As these are the deceased person's belongings, it's their call.

Either way, clients should be aware that the generations coming after them are increasingly disinclined to receive all that silverware and fine china they've been storing for years. Tastes have changed. While there are certainly still collectibles that have value, the list is shrinking. Few people would say no to inheriting a coin collection or valuable artwork, or even a sentimental item, such as the perfectly seasoned cast iron frying pan that reminds one of family gatherings with their grandmother's cooking. But most people just don't have the space to keep all the other hand-me-downs they will never use.

No, there are worse things a person can do than leave a junk pile. The most frustrating, of course, is not leaving a will or leaving a will that no one can find. Among the list of frustrations might also be the decedent not creating an inventory of their assets or a list of the institutions associated with those assets. This will leave the fiduciary in the role of a forensic scientist trying to figure out what their estate includes. Professional trustees and corporate fiduciaries could provide a litany of other examples, given they do the job of estate administration for a living. The next worst thing is the decedent leaving the fiduciary and beneficiaries in the dark about their digital life and digital assets.

Estate Planning and Estate Administration Conversations

We enjoy technology in our lives, but digital assets become difficult to access after incapacity or death. The digital world has become very relevant in estate planning for two simple reasons. First, people may have preferences about what they want done with their digital lives. Those considerations are exactly the same as for their physical property or property rights. Second, people will definitely need to leave some information behind for the fiduciary on where to find their digital possessions and what they expect them to do. The big difference with digital possessions is that they are just a little trickier to find if the deceased doesn't leave a list of what they have, and it can be next to impossible to do anything with them if they haven't pre-planned. Additionally, the testator may have preferences about their digital life that are different for their incapacity versus their death.

Practically and technically speaking, without a password, all of the cybersecurity and privacy measures put in place to protect oneself from identity theft, hacking, and cybertheft of one's accounts will be barriers for the fiduciary. Even if the fiduciary has the legal right to access the testator's accounts in their jurisdiction, passwords can get written down incorrectly or expire. In terms of technology, process, and the functionality of today's software, it may still be difficult in some cases for the fiduciary to gain access, even with a password. Testators would be well advised to consider other pre-planning options.

To illustrate how one's digital life has already affected their estate planning, compare a testator's home office today to what it looked like back in the 1980s.

What would a fiduciary likely have found in the home office of a deceased person in the 1980s? If they were lucky, they would have found an estate binder or even a file folder with an inventory of all the estate assets and other supporting information, such as pensions, insurance policies, and funeral pre-arrangements. While we had information technology back then, most people likely kept hard copy records and left a paper trail that would have been relatively easy to follow. The Rolodex or address book would have been helpful in providing names and contact information of key people in their life, such as family, beneficiaries, and friends to call to attend the funeral, or those they would have dealt with professionally, such as their tax advisor. While it might not have been all that neat and tidy, the fiduciary at least had a fighting chance of collecting the necessary paperwork about the estate, beyond what would have been in the will.

Today's fiduciary will walk into the deceased's home office and likely mutter under their breath, "Please, please, please, let there be an estate binder or at least a printed copy of some statements that are not shredded." And to their surprise, a disembodied voice responds from ceiling speakers connected to a home digital assistant:

> Hey you, fiduciary. I am the digital assistant. No, sorry, Ms. Privacy didn't create an estate binder. She had planned to but used the time to set me up instead—she told me it was more fun than collecting paperwork. Oh, and good luck finding any passwords that will give you access to her laptop and other electronic devices: they were written on a small note taped under the desk, but it fell to the floor and someone got it stuck under their shoe and walked off with it several months ago.

Even paper shredders have gotten more technologically advanced. The fiduciary might have been able to rescue the long strips of paper from older shredders from the recycling bin and taped them together like you see in the movies. But no, now we all buy crosscut paper shredders as though we're concerned a SWAT team is going to appear at any moment. Kidding aside, I am aware of the privacy, security, and confidentiality reasons to shred documents with personal information when recycling.

Today's fiduciary might locate an estate binder with an inventory of the deceased's assets and other supporting information; however, if the deceased has gone paperless and everything is on digital files somewhere, the fiduciary could be in big trouble. Without passwords, they will not be able to turn on the deceased's device and go through their digital or online files, or even peruse the contact list on a smartphone. And if the deceased has been avidly shredding their financial statements and other documents to keep paper from proliferating or for security concerns, the fiduciary could be in a predicament.

Whereas financial institutions have made it easier for a fiduciary with the right paperwork to obtain information, the fiduciary needs to know which financial institution to go to, whether it's a traditional brick-and-mortar bank, an online-only operation, a global bank, or a grocery store that offers banking. That doesn't even begin to cover all the possibilities for insurance companies, wealth management firms, and the other endless financial management possibilities. If the fiduciary does not know what institutions their client deals with, it's not unreasonable that they could be faced with making dozens or hundreds of cold calls to figure out where the client holds accounts or assets.

The push to go paperless doesn't stop there: utilities (e.g., water, power, gas), telephone, internet and cable television providers, retailers and more are all driving their customers online, either directly or via their bank. It makes sense. Online transactions save paper and postage. However, this digital trail doesn't necessarily leave many clues for the fiduciary to follow. With no paper trail, it may be more difficult for the fiduciary to find their client's assets so that they can begin shutting down services they will no longer be using.

This work can add to the estate administration costs and, in the worst-case scenario, result in assets that languish, unclaimed, dormant, and unused in cyberspace. Want proof? Go online to any unclaimed property registry in your jurisdiction and for fun look up your own name.

At the end of 2020, on the Bank of Canada's Unclaimed Balances portal there was a staggering 2.3 million unclaimed balances worth CAD$973 million. Another example is the US Federal Government web page Unclaimed Money from the Government, which has convenient links to search for unclaimed money from one's state (or multi-state), as well as unclaimed money from insurance, tax refunds, employers, and other sources.

It doesn't stop there. Some jurisdictions have further unclaimed property laws to hold onto uncollected assets for years—assets such as unclaimed wages or commissions, or dormant accounts. Some have searchable databases, like the one operated by the British Columbia Unclaimed Property Society (BCUPS). I learned of BCUPS when one of my university colleagues asked me to look at a letter he had received from this entity. The letter stated that BCUPS was holding money for him from his time at university 20 years ago and asked him to provide some personal information to make a claim. Rightly so, in this day and age, he thought the letter was a fraud and called the university payroll department directly to determine if the letter was legitimate. It turned out to be true, and he collected enough money for a dinner out with his family. I applauded my friend for being skeptical and taking a couple of minutes to make a few extra phone calls to verify, independently, that the letter was valid.

While it may seem like a throwback to the pre-internet world, a good old-fashioned binder with actual paper in it still has a role in estate planning. Go ahead and also include a flash drive, a CD/DVD, memory stick, or other storage device, as additional backup and leave it with the binder. However, as technology advances, there is nothing wrong with printing a hard copy of important documents—and it might prove to be invaluable. Remember when floppy disks were the norm? Perhaps a flash drive might be extinct when you pass away. It could leave the fiduciary on the hunt for a relic or old-school device to review your information, only to find that the media doesn't work because it was too old or became corrupted.

Individuals should be concerned about the confidentiality of all the information in an estate binder and take precautions. Advise clients to lock it in a file cabinet or safety deposit box, or ask the legal advisor for other recommended options for securing the binder. Again, ensure the fiduciary knows how they can get at it when they need to. For financial-related information, a much more secure approach is to list only the names of the institutions dealt with, their phone numbers, addresses, and perhaps a contact person. Omit all the account numbers and any financial data entirely. Creating this simple list, without account or financial data, is light years ahead of what most people do, and it's all the fiduciary needs. The fiduciary could then go to the specific institutions and get the additional information when required. This list ideally would include bills, debts, and liabilities. When it comes to bills, such as utility bills and subscriptions, providing the address where the services are delivered, if different from the mailing or invoicing address, along with the name of the person on the account, will help the fiduciary. Even if the account doesn't involve any financial holdings or data, including the account number or account type will help the fiduciary when closing the account.

A New Language

The term digital assets is just not that client-friendly, and a client is likely to think it has something to do with Millennials or cryptoassets. I tell clients that digital assets are their memories, their money, and their records, just now in digital form instead of on paper. Digital assets are assets a client owns, has rights to use (by holding a license) that involve technology or are digitized. They could be stored electronically on a device such as a personal computer, laptop, tablet, or smartphone, or online. There are several terms used to describe digital assets, including *digital property*, *virtual assets*, *digital files*, *intangible assets*, *intangible personal property*, *technological assets*, *paperless assets*, *cyberassets*, *cryptoassets*, *electronic records*, *electronically stored information*, or *electronic communication*.

Of course, for your own clinical advisory purposes, you'll want to refer to your own jurisdiction-specific legal definition. Two model law examples:

The Uniform Law Conference of Canada, *Uniform Access to Digital Assets by Fiduciaries Act* (2016): "*A digital asset may be defined as anything that is stored in a binary format or more simply an electronic record.*" The Introduction to the Act defines a digital asset as follows: "*digital asset means a record that is created,*

51

recorded, transmitted or stored in digital or other intangible form by electronic, magnetic or optical means or by any other similar means ..."

The Uniform Law Commission (USA), as per Prefatory Note, *Fiduciary Access to Digital Assets Act*, Revised (2015): *"Digital asset are electronic records in which individuals have a right or interest."*

Adam Steen, a leading academic in the digital assets space who is on the STEP Academy and Digital Assets SIG, indicates in the *Financial Planning Research Journal* that *"digital assets can be said to include any assets that can be accessed and held online in digital form."*

When I'm asked to describe the characteristics of a digital asset, my answer includes the following:

- It is something in a digital format.
- It likely needs some hardware and a power source to access.
- It can have some value or utility to you, just the way a physical asset can.
- It won't work well if it is not maintained, secured, or backed up.
- Good luck accessing it if you lost your password and had not previously set up a recovery process.

Regardless of what they are called or how they are categorized, what is relevant to estate planning, according to STEP, is that digital assets *"may be of financial or sentimental value to you and your family. They can be as precious and important as physical assets that you can touch."*

Digital assets may also provide access to something physical, such as a financial holding (known as an *underlying asset*, such as a bank account or stock account), or have privacy considerations (clients may think of the privacy setting on their social media accounts, but privacy applies to all accounts), or contain information about their identity that they'll want protected from identity theft.

One further complication to add to the mix are tangible assets such as digital devices. With the proliferation of cloud-based services, most hardware is reduced to being just a conduit to data stored in the cloud.

The technology space seems to include a variety of terms used to describe the company providing technology products or services, whether they are free or paid-for services (e.g., technology provider, software business, software provider, service provider, social media platform provider, software vendor, business, hosting provider, hardware vendor, software platform provider, and third-party technology provider). As indicated, I refer to businesses providing technology-related services or products as *service providers* (e.g., technology providers, e-mail providers, and software providers).

Digital assets often require access to information, meaning users often need to provide some form of protected digital information to gain access: a username, log-in information, an e-mail address, a digital key, a public key, or user credentials, along with a password, a personal identification number, and/or private key. Digital access information can also include additional service provider multi-factor verification. To simplify, I'll refer to the digital assets that require digital access as needing a password. Digital access to digital assets after incapacity and/or death needs a re-think. Passwords and password managers were designed for the living, and do not take into consideration the requirements of the estate business process and of the client.

Why Are Your Client's Digital Assets Important in Estate Planning?

Estate planning of our digital lives is a new aspect of will/estate planning and incapacity planning, followed by estate administration for the fiduciary. Estate planning of our digital assets has become a topic of importance to STEP, whereas they launched a new membership category, the Friends of STEP, for those in other professions associated with the estate industry, such as service providers.

Clients' digital assets are important in estate planning for all the reasons their non-digital or physical assets are. First, they may have preferences about what happens to these assets after their death, and those wishes need to be documented and communicated just as they would for their non-digital assets. Second, there are some similarities and differences between physical assets and digital assets that are worth examining, as it can impact how clients handle these assets in terms of estate planning, or what the fiduciary can actually do during estate administration.

For example, a client wanting to leave their online music or movie collection to their children might not be able to. If a client purchased and downloaded music or movies, only they likely have a licence to the files, which means they can use them but might not be able to transfer them to someone else. Clients should check the licensing agreement or terms of service. Leaving this legacy might be less of a concern if they opted not to download but instead used a streaming service, where users pay a monthly fee with no expectations that anything can be transferred. This example demonstrates how quickly things are changing in the technology space.

The estate planning and estate administration of digital assets follows a similar process as non-digital assets. The key activities of estate planning, such as documenting one's wishes and plans, are exactly the same as for digital assets. These activities can include clients providing instructions for inclusion in their will. Clients may be familiar with some of the key activities that the fiduciary will have to do in estate administration. These activities are exactly the same for digital assets:

- Finding, securing, and creating an inventory of assets
- Closing accounts, paying debts, and paying expenses
- Assessing the value of assets, applying some post-mortem tax planning
- Distributing assets according to the will

Borrowing from the technology toolkit, I often find it useful when I help a client plan their technology project to look at a client's processes and ask: what is the same and what is different? If we know what is the same, then perhaps we can use a similar approach to deal with digital assets as for any other assets in estate planning. Understanding the differences between physical and digital also allows the client to deal with these characteristics directly in planning. Perhaps then the client can figure out a new approach or engage new expertise to help them with the things that are different. The same principle will also apply to the fiduciary handling a client's digital assets: the characteristics of digital assets, in their similarities and differences to physical assets, will affect what they do.

Some of the Similarities May Be Surprising

- Digital assets may have financial value. Clients may have an e-book, generate advertising revenue from a social media channel or blog, sell their art or photographs online, or run an online business. Cryptocurrencies or cryptoassets have certainly raised the awareness of the financial value of digital assets. As another example, some websites and domain names can have value. During the tech boom of the early 2000s rumors of million-dollar URLs were not uncommon. A website or domain name your client owns could represent financial value if there is a buyer willing to pay for it.

- Digital assets may have sentimental or emotional value. Users don't often think of giving their technology a hug or that it will hug them back. The idea here is that, for now, digital assets may hold sentimental value, such as digital photographs, but wait for virtual reality, artificial intelligence, and robotics to become mainstream in the home. What happens then?

- Some of the legal aspects that apply to physical property may also apply to digital assets. Your e-book or digital photographs may be subject to laws such as intellectual property rights (e.g., copyright) or have royalty attributes.

- Digital assets have privacy, security, and/or confidentiality considerations; i.e., who do clients want reading their e-mail? Or perhaps they have preferences for what to do with their social media accounts (keep them open or close them).

- Digital assets can have tax attributes. If they have a financial value, there could be a tax liability.

- The fiduciary may need specialized help (e.g., technical, legal, or tax) to deal with digital assets in estate administration.

Some Key Differences

- Some digital assets can be physically undetectable. This could include e-mail accounts, online subscriptions, or social media accounts. A fiduciary needs to know what their client has, as these likely won't turn up in a physical search of their house.

- As internet and platform users, we use passwords to access most online accounts. When passwords are required, and they typically are (no password often means no access), what then? I find it interesting that people are sometimes under the delusion that somehow the password will magically reappear, or they'll get their password reset, but it just doesn't happen that easily anymore, thanks to preventative measures put in place to counter cybercrime.

- The value of digital assets can diminish over time. This means the fiduciary might not have a lot of time to extract the value of a digital asset before it devalues or expires.

- Ownership rights are one of the biggies. Many online accounts, software platforms, or digital assets that clients think they are buying are actually only licensed, governed by licensing agreements or contracts. Remember signing up for that account and reading, scrolling through, and agreeing to a litany of information before getting access? That contract between the user and the company is sometimes called a *licensing agreement, terms of use agreement, or terms of service agreement (TOSA)*. They differ from one company to the next, but some don't allow the user to give their digital access to anyone else. The big surprise here is that the user may not actually own the digital assets they have signed up for, or they may be limited or prohibited from passing them along. For many digital assets, ownership or the licensing arrangement may end on death and/or transferring title may be restricted or prohibited altogether.

- Fiduciaries will need to confirm they have a legal right to access their client's digital assets or online accounts in their jurisdiction.

- Location of the digital asset in law (called *situs*) may be more challenging to determine than that of a physical asset because it's virtual.

- Privacy, confidentially, and security are concerns for some physical assets, but these are paramount when dealing with digital assets.

In summary, identifying the similarities and differences between physical and digital assets aids us in understanding this new topic relative to things we already comprehend. You don't need to get too concerned about whether a characteristic is different or not. What is truly important are the characteristics themselves and how to work with them, and then how to help the fiduciary administer the assets when the time comes.

The Practical Crux of the Digital Conversation

Now that we have become a little more comfortable with the

characteristics of digital assets, let's explore the practical crux of the matter in dealing with the digital realm. I'll illustrate with this example: Say your client has an apartment. Your client dies, and no one seems to be able to find a set of keys to the apartment. The fiduciary, named in the client's will, would likely first ask the client's family members. Unfortunately, none of them has a key. Then, armed with the original will or proof of probate, the fiduciary would ask the apartment manager to open the door. The apartment manager will see that the legal document gives the fiduciary the authority and will comply by providing a set of keys. The fiduciary is using the authority granted by law to gain access to that apartment.

Now, if the apartment manager was away, and it was urgent to gain access to the apartment, the fiduciary could call a locksmith. The fiduciary would show the proof of probate to the locksmith and use the authority of the will to hire the locksmith. They might be able to gain access because they could use their magic drills and special tools. So, in the case of this physical asset, the law can help the fiduciary to gain access through using an expert to open the door.

Under the digital umbrella, let's talk about the client's computer (as a digital device or hardware). Let us say the client left wishes that the photos on their computer were to be given to their children, but the client forgot to leave instructions on where the fiduciary could retrieve the password to the computer.

The fiduciary wastes time looking and has no luck, so they decide to go to a computer store for help. Their chances in gaining access to the data on your computer are really going to be, at best, a roll of the dice. The deceased's proof of computer ownership will have to be verified. Did the client leave the receipt with the serial number, proving that it is theirs? The fiduciary, even with the proof of probate, will need to prove that this computer is the client's. This situation is no different than a client's claims that they own a specific asset, such as a car. The fiduciary can only deal with that asset if the vehicle ownership permit is in the client's name.

The computer store, like the apartment manager, will recognize the authority of the proof of probate and try to help the fiduciary. Unfortunately, they may not physically be able to get into that computer and access the data, especially if the hard drive was encrypted. Much of the technology we use today has been hardened to prevent access by hackers and cybercriminals and to protect the user's privacy. Can fiduciaries use their authority under the law to open that laptop? Probably not, because it might be really locked down, with no magic drill or special tool to get into some computers or encrypted data.

A user may want to give the computer to someone, with the idea that they would load their own data on it, so they would own it and use it for themselves. Some computer hardware can be reset without a password. All the data and programs previously on it will be wiped out. For many people, the data on the computer, those digital assets such as photos and other artifacts, are what are really important.

Does technology have a back door? Yes and no. It depends on the provider. There is one additional challenge: Even if there's a back door, will the company that created it allow the fiduciary access? There might be procedures and paperwork for the fiduciary to fill out. Even then, they might not gain access if the licensing agreement prevents them, or if the company does not comply for privacy, jurisdictional law, or some other reason.

The law might not be enough to get into that computer, and that is the practical crux of the digital assets matter.

Client Conversations: Digital Assets Inventories

The STEP Digital Assets Global Special Interest Group has created several guidance documents that estate advisors can use with their clients in estate planning discussions to deal with digital assets. One of the guides, the *Inventory for Digital Assets and Digital Devices* ("STEP Inventory"), aids advisors in having conversations with their clients and encouraging them to document the digital assets in their lives. Note, this inventory also recommends that the digital access information (e.g., passwords) is not stored as part of the inventory. STEP also offers additional information and a *Digital Assets Public Guide* with information to help with pre-planning questions such as, What are my digital assets and why are my digital assets important?

When discussing a digital assets inventory with a client, keep in mind that the client may not be as familiar with the terms discussed in the death positive, death care, and estate industries, which are not as well known as financial literacy terms. It's helpful to cover the what's what first, so we know what we are talking about in the context of estate planning. For example, a basic death literacy concept is that a client may have preferences upon incapacity and/or death concerning their property, digital or otherwise.

As discussed, a digital asset is simply our money, our memories, and our records that are now in digital form instead of on paper. Anything we do online involves electronic records and is relevant in estate planning and estate administration. As mentioned earlier in this chapter, STEP considers that digital assets may have the same financial or sentimental value as our physical assets. We have some of the same emotional attachments to the elements of our digital footprint as we do to physical items.

Why would someone need a digital assets inventory? Creating an inventory is a basic first step in will and estate planning. The word *assets*, another estate industry term, generally refers to the things the client owns or has rights to. Advisors and estate planners ask clients about their wishes, preferences, and intentions regarding their beneficiaries—this scope of questioning should include digital as well as physical assets and rights. But the estate planning equation is more holistic than just wills and inventories, considering client legacy wishes, charitable and philanthropic wishes, advance care planning, taxes, insurance, funerals, financial planning, and other end-of-life considerations. Then there are the endless amounts of approaches, depending on the client's circumstances. But if we get to the nuts and bolts of some of the process elements, traditionally that list or inventory was just about physical assets or property rights, such as bank accounts, homes, coin collections, photo albums, or mementos.

Estate planners have long advised to create an estate binder, folder, or simply a piece of paper with information for their fiduciary. Ideally, this binder or document summarizes the estate plan, giving enough information for beneficiaries and fiduciaries to execute on the decedent's wishes, avoiding a detective effort after the fact. The digital assets inventory is an extension of their physical inventory or estate binder, now including all the digital aspects of their life.

The STEP Inventory was first published in 2017. Subsequently, I led the SIG committee revisions team and published a revised version in September 2020. Although it was written as a tool for advisors to share with clients, it was also written with the tech industry in mind. The STEP Inventory is organized in three main parts: Section One is for digital assets, those pure electronic records; Section Two is for digital devices, the physical devices we use, such as tablets and computers; and Section Three is for digital accounts, online accounts used to access underlying assets such as bank accounts, home management accounts, and loyalty points.

Version 2.0 of the document provides additional questions to help guide the client in building their inventory with tips for handling every digital asset type. The document is for individual or household planning; additional information would be required for business or organizational entities with business interests.

Here are two examples of guidance from the STEP Inventory provides to illustrate that not all digital assets are planned for and handled in the same way:

> "Social Media Platforms: Social Media Tip—Look for and/ or ask for provider pre-planning options. For example, Facebook Legacy Contact has the option to select either memorialise or delete an account (search in setting or

help). If you select a person other than your fiduciary as Legacy Contact, let the fiduciary know."

Social Media is a new item from an estate planning perspective with its own norms for individuals and the estate industry to consider, although some estate planning concepts will be the same, such as letting beneficiaries and fiduciaries know of these designations. The idea that an individual might pick someone other than their fiduciary is similar to picking a beneficiary for an insurance policy.

> "Underlying Assets: Online Account Tip—Password sharing is prohibited for most if not all online accounts. Refer to the terms of service and/or jurisdiction-specific laws. Contact each institution to determine if any advance planning or registration is available, such as registering the fiduciary or providing separate secure and compliant access. Ask what information can be shared in advance with the fiduciary."

Sometimes we forget that there are individuals at businesses behind the screen when our interface is entirely online, but we can reach out to customer service for in-person or chat-based help. For example, if a fiduciary is appointed in a power-of-attorney document, trust, deed, or will, that fiduciary should not be using the client's log-in and password details, they should be reaching out to the institution the client deals with to secure their own credentials or make other arrangements as appropriate to the situation.

The STEP Inventory, currently 20 pages long, is intended to be an all-encompassing point-in-time tool and used to capture one's digital footprint as it grows. Recognizing it can be overwhelming to consider one's own personal digital assets inventory, STEP also recommends identifying the top-most important digital assets, which if lost would be devastating to the testator or will-maker.

The STEP Inventory encourages individuals to consider documenting their digital lives as well as their physical lives in the will and estate planning process. But documentation doesn't end with the inventory. You'll want to advise the client to wrap any legal, tax, or other estate planning considerations and instructions around it. In addition, from a tech management perspective, there could be other detailed plans, pre-planning steps, and information required to successfully transfer a digital asset upon incapacity and/or death.

Tech entrepreneurs have been on the scene for several years creating what the *STEP Journal* article refers to as *digital asset administration tools (digital vaults)*. In the past year, I've seen an explosion of choices for digital asset vaults for one's traditional physical inventory as well as estate administration products. As the estate industry digitizes, we'll see a number of solutions and more integrated platforms that cover the estate planning, incapacity planning and estate administration processes.

Executor Conversations: Digital Executors

The term *digital executor* is made up. In some respects, there is no such thing as a digital executor, any more than there is an art executor, house executor, or a specific asset executor, other than the named executor or fiduciary(s) in the will, or the power(s) someone gives to another specifically in the will. Using the term *digital executor* to raise awareness of the expanding role of the fiduciary is great. However, we need to be careful on the terminology.

Accounting for digital assets has become relevant in estate planning. The big difference with digital assets is they are trickier to find if clients don't leave a list, and difficult to manage if clients don't plan ahead, create technical management plans, have a backup plan, or leverage any provider pre-planning functionality that is offered. So, the idea that a client's one and only fiduciary might need some help if they are not tech savvy is relevant. Keep in mind, though, that not all digital assets need someone to be computer literate. For example, for access to a client's bank account, the fiduciary should go to the financial institution directly, and not use the client's credentials and log in to their online bank account.

Newsflash! Our digital and non-digital lives are very much inter-twined. Suppose a client has an online newspaper subscription and wants (or expects) that subscription to be cancelled after they die. Further, suppose the client considers two different people are involved in their estate, namely a digital executor and an execu-tor, or a digital fiduciary and a fiduciary. Which fiduciary would the client choose to deal with this online newspaper subscription? I would suggest that, just as one would have expected for a physical newspaper, the client would want their fiduciary to deal with that. If all the client's information on their physical assets (underlying assets) are managed through digital assets in an online account, then having someone called a digital fiduciary is potentially giving away some, or all, of the fiduciary's role. It could certainly cause confusion over who is responsible for dealing with what.

Perhaps clients should keep it simple. One consideration is that the fiduciary will have this extra job and should treat digital assets just like any other asset class. If the fiduciary isn't computer-lit-erate, the client might want to consider what additional informa-tion to leave behind to support them, and also encourage them to seek qualified technical help or qualified advisory support. This is the same way a client might expect the fiduciary to engage an art dealer or an art appraiser when dealing with an art collection or engage a real estate agent when dealing with selling a home. The fiduciary will be expected to vet expert options, select the exper-tise they need, oversee their work, and confirm that the work was done in the manner they expected.

Seeking legal advice and including digital assets within the will is critical as is the language to address wishes and preferences for digital assets, along with the responsibilities of the fiduciary. Clients will want legal advice and perhaps legal drafting in a situ-ation where there are specifically identified digital assets of sig-nificance that they want handled in a specific way with a specific person or persons who is not the named fiduciary.

From a practical perspective, if the client decides they want to appoint someone called a digital fiduciary or digital advisor, and this person is different from their named fiduciary, I suggest they identify which digital assets each individual is responsible for, review the powers assigned, outline how conflicts will be dealt with, and seek legal advice. In some respects, it is no different than assigning someone powers to deal with a physical asset; it is no different for digital assets: both categories require being precise on the extent of the powers assigned.

From a project planning point of view, given where things stand today, a blanket statement that says a digital fiduciary is to deal with digital assets, and the fiduciary is to deal with everything else can seem a tidy way to do this. However, I believe not pre-planning these role assignments or contemplating the impact of not doing so could create confusion during estate administration. There could be lots of overlap.

Here are some estate administration questions the scenario of two fiduciaries generates:

- If a computer is a physical asset (it is not considered a digital asset because it is not an electronic record), but the files stored on it are digital assets, what then? Who does what?
- Is the estate going to pay the digital fiduciary? Shutting down an easy account might take minutes and a few clicks of a button, but what if there are many complex accounts?
- What if the digital fiduciary spends considerable time just trying to figure out what the digital assets are?
- Physical assets can take time, in terms of getting an appraisal, finding a market, and evaluating bids, not to mention all the supporting contracting to make these tasks happen. The same can apply to digital assets. Whose job is to sell a web domain belonging to an estate?
- What if the digital fiduciary makes a mistake that affects the rest of the estate?
- What if the digital fiduciary has expenses in carrying out their assigned tasks? For security and/or privacy reasons, they may require separate internet access or other technical tools to do the job.

- What if the digital fiduciary needs to hire professional help, incurring costs to the estate, because they need technical support or legal advice?
- Who oversees the work of the digital fiduciary?
- Would the digital fiduciary know they shouldn't access an underlying financial asset?
- What if the digital fiduciary is handling assets that have financial value? Are they supposed to engage a tax advisor and complete tax forms?

Client/Executor Conversations: Digital Assets

Have the client begin by creating a digital assets inventory. They should leave digital access information in a separate, secure location in a manner that does not attract legal or criminal liability, review any provider agreements, research provider guidance, test access instructions, and then advise the fiduciary on how to access.

What will be acceptable as digital access information for the fiduciary is an evolving space. From a practical perspective, giving someone a list of passwords without guidance is as dangerous as leaving your car keys in the ignition or dropping your wallet on the street. Worse, in fact, because passwords in the wrong hands or accidentally mishandled can cause enormous damage to the client's bottom line, identity, and reputation. From a project management perspective, the client can prepare the fiduciary by reviewing with them what needs to be done in a little more detail, regarding their various digital assets. Refer to Chapter Five for more insights into taking a project management approach in the role of a fiduciary. Before having the conversation with the fiduciary, clients will want to review their digital assets inventory and wishes with their legal advisor and ask if a digital asset clause in their will is appropriate for their situation. Questions for a legal advisor include if the fiduciary has the legal right to access the testator's digital assets after death, what jurisdictional laws cover the fiduciary's role, and what specific digital assets may pose a challenge based on where they are located or because of licensing agreements.

Legal Conversations: Laws Will Need to Catch Up

As with most technological innovation, lawmakers often need to play catch-up, by either updating legislation or creating new laws, such as will be the case for digital assets. There will be a number of questions for the law to tackle with respect to digital assets such as, What is the legal definition of digital property versus other types of digital assets? What is and isn't digital property that you own? Who can access your digital property? The law would also have to tackle pre- and post-mortem privacy issues and differing jurisdictional laws.

How does one deal with a digital asset that has other laws involved (e.g., intellectual property law, business law, privacy law, contract law, other jurisdictional laws, conflict of laws)? Some technology providers now allow users to identify a contact for pre-planning of digital assets, but how does this role mesh with the fiduciary role, and how will the law deal with conflict? Is the fiduciary responsible for only digital property or all digital assets? What are the differences in handling digital assets between a fiduciary named as the power of attorney or a court-appointed guardian and the fiduciary who assumes the role of executor or estate trustee named in the will or the role of administrator if there is no will?

One particularly new area is the powers of the fiduciary in handling digital assets in a specific jurisdiction. What the fiduciary is allowed to do is covered by jurisdictional laws of either the place where the deceased or incapacitated person resides or the situs where the digital asset is located. The laws in every country are different, and in some cases, dramatically so.

As outlined in Chapter One the majority of US states have adopted a form of RUFADAA, which states that the fiduciary can't access certain kinds of digital assets or the contents of a deceased person's accounts governed by terms of service agreements, unless the deceased person had given explicit approval while they were alive.

However, what the US does legislatively just might affect us globally in some situations—consider where some of the big technology companies are located. Suppose the fiduciary has to go knocking on the provider's US door because they were locked out of the deceased's account. Such a scenario, based on the specific provider and a set of specific circumstances, becomes a matter for legal advisors pertaining to conflict of law to address and far beyond the scope of this introductory topic. Let us leave it at this: Given how relatively new this subject is, any fiduciary, regardless of jurisdiction, should be very careful about using an incapacitated or deceased person's password and should engage legal advice on how to approach this new digital territory before they begin.

Fiduciaries Should Proceed With Caution in Dealing With Digital Assets

As things stand, a prudent fiduciary should be careful when dealing with the digital assets of a deceased person. They should be encouraged to begin by creating a proposed digital assets estate administration plan for dealing with these assets. This plan could include the following activities:

- Create a list of the digital assets they find.
- Evaluate how to secure them.
- Review the will.
- Review any other supporting documents.
- Review the licensing agreements.
- Research digital assets providers for guidance or cautionary statements.
- Determine which digital assets provide digital access to an underlying asset (e.g., bank account), which the fiduciary should not have accessed online.
- Determine if the value needs to be assessed.
- Determine if other expertise is required.
- Find any tax information.

- Detail any proposed actions for accessing, securing, transferring, or disposing of assets.

I then recommend fiduciaries seek legal advice on their proposed plans to access, secure, transfer, or dispose of the digital assets. Then, while in the throes of estate administration, if a fiduciary encounters challenges dealing with a particularly difficult digital asset, they should re-engage a legal advisor. Similar to other assets, if managing digital assets gets complicated, they can also apply to the court for direction. For example, they may have questions about their ability to access a specific asset or how the law would interpret the deceased person's ownership rights of that asset.

A Reminder That Client Digital Assets Affect Businesses Supporting the Estate Industry

As stated in Chapter One, technology is the new player at the client's estate planning table. As the laws catch up, businesses supporting the estate industry, such as law firms, trust companies, and financial institutions will also need to update their policies and processes to deal with digital assets. For a professional fiduciary, such as a trust company, this will be a new world, with updates needed to their technology management policies, practices, and tools to include handling a client's digital assets.

For example, for security reasons, most businesses don't allow any outside devices (such as the one owned by the deceased) to be plugged into their network, nor do they allow anyone other than their employees to access their internet connection. As such, dealing with a client's digital assets is everything that a firm's information technology department wouldn't want you to do on their network. Separate protected environments may need to be set up or outsourced to third-party technology providers to deal with digital assets.

The technology industry and businesses interacting with clients online have also yet to catch up to some of the requirements of the estate planning and estate administration fields in dealing with digital assets. Few companies have processes in place to allow users to select preferences for closing or transferring their accounts after they are deceased. Some of us will be familiar with the heartbreaking stories of families dealing with tragic deaths who had to go to court to petition for access to the online accounts of their loved ones. The future is going to get even trickier: How do you leave behind your biometric passwords, such as retinal scans or fingerprints? We can't, so we need other legally and contractually compliant estate transfer options for digital assets. At some point, the market (meaning all of us as shareholders, clients, and consumers) will pressure the technology industry to provide better options allowing people to securely leave their digital assets to their beneficiaries either directly or through a fiduciary, and those options will need to be integrated with the law.

Digital Assets and Taxes

Some digital assets have taxable attributes, so when assets are deemed disposed of, or the fiduciary sells or transfers them, there could be tax implications. In essence, digital assets are treated exactly like regular assets. For example, if the client owns a valuable internet web domain that can be sold, the fiduciary not only needs to know about it, but also will need to know the amount paid for it and the expenses associated with it, in order to calculate capital gains, if that is the tax treatment for that specific asset. Similarly, for other assets, the client should seek tax advice for estate planning of digital assets of financial value.

As for cryptocurrencies, many people wonder if they are taxable when sold. The short answer is yes. How they are taxed, specifically, will depend on a number of factors, including jurisdiction. For example, there are some techies out there who receive cryptocurrencies because they mine them (i.e., they receive cryptocurrency as revenue or business income). Cryptocurrency received as revenue or business income may be used for buying or selling, used to pay for products or services, used as remuneration to employees, or used by a speculative investor. The tax treatment may vary depending on the usage of the cryptocurrency. How cryptocurrency is treated in a particular circumstance can only be established by a tax advisor or the appropriate tax authority.

Privacy and Estate Planning

The use of digital assets in everyday life can undermine estate planning objectives. Suppose the client has a cousin, Mr. Privacy. Every time the client gets together with Mr. Privacy, he shares his main concern about protecting his and his family's privacy, as he owns a small business where most of his family works. Mr. Privacy, through estate planning, after discussing the various options with his estate advisors, decides to move his assets into a family trust for privacy reasons and succession planning. When your client asked Mr. Privacy why he set up a family trust, his answer was that his primary motivation for the family trust was to protect his privacy—he did not want his family's net worth and his personal holdings to become public record. To do so, Mr. Privacy hired estate legal and tax advisors, spent considerable time and effort on the trust deed, then paid the transaction fees required to constitute this trust relationship.

Mr. Privacy also spends considerable effort to remain low-key in his business dealings. In fact, although he is the owner of a small business, he enlisted a company spokesperson to deal with all the public-facing aspects of his business. Mr. Privacy is not very tech savvy, and his marketing director has been urging him to create a social media profile for his business, which he has ignored.

Let's check what is happening in Mr. Privacy's personal life. Mr. Privacy, at some point, was introduced to social media by his grandson, who created his profile. He now loves keeping up with family and friends on social media, but what Mr. Privacy doesn't realize is that his privacy settings are open to the world.

Social media accounts offer a variety of privacy and security options, depending on the provider, starting with the amount of information you provide in your profile. Consider these standard settings:

- The first one is open to the world, very public.

  - Anyone with an internet-connected device can look up the user's name and look at the user's information, posts, and photos.
  - Do you ever wonder why news reports often include a social media photo of the reported person? The journalist went to various social media sites and downloaded that photo. You'll see the credit in the photo caption in small print.

- The next level of privacy setting allows users to select specific people to see their profile and their content.

- The third level lets users apply even more restrictions on who can see what aspects of their content within their social network.

So now let us examine what the world knows about Mr. Privacy through his social media accounts that anyone around the world could access:

- He posts photos of all his real property because he loves taking pictures of all his family events.
- His children and grandchildren post pictures of all the vacations they have been on and photos of his pets and prized possessions.
- Mr. Privacy's friends congratulate him on his various company successes.
- His grandson follows him around taking pictures of the inside of his place of business.

Let's just consider these digital photos for one moment. Because they are digital, the file contains additional embedded information called metadata (i.e., what kind of device took the picture, the location where the photo was taken, and the date the photo was taken). So now anyone can know exactly where those photos were taken, what Mr. Privacy owns, and where he lives. Depending on how long Mr. Privacy has been posting information, anyone can create a pretty good picture of his life.

The client's cousin, Mr. Privacy, has now undermined his primary objective of privacy, simply by the way he failed to secure his one social media account.

Cybercrime and identity theft have become rampant; every other day, there seems to be a story of yet another company that got hacked. Cyberthieves not only prey upon those who are vulnerable or incapacitated, but also readily target those that are fully capable but lax in protecting their digital assets and guarding their online presence. I suggest your clients consider their home technology, digital assets, and digital access information as they would any other important home appliance or valuable assets. They should exercise the same care and attention to research when they purchase technology, seek qualified help to set up their devices correctly, read the company's advice on their use, review the user manual, and spend the time and money required to maintain and secure them properly. This area, quite frankly, is something all of us need to get better at understanding, protecting, and maintaining, if we truly want to use technology sustainably in our lives in the long term. Technology can seem advanced, magical, and maintenance free, but it is not.

Technology providers offer guidance on how to protect the user's digital assets and protect their family in an online, connected world. The usual advice begins with the following:

- Adopt advanced digital access practices (e.g., strong passwords and additional authentication methods) for all accounts and devices.
- Delete accounts, e-mails, and content that are no longer required.
- Regularly review the privacy settings on your accounts and devices.
- Don't open documents or click on links in suspicious e-mails or, better yet, don't click on links at all—go to known websites directly.

- Only visit reputable businesses or websites online.
- Regularly update hardware and software.
- Use a virtual private network (VPN) to encrypt internet traffic.
- Encrypt the data on all your devices.
- Have at least two backups of important data.
- Use virus and malware removal and protection software.
- Double down on protective measures when introducing younger people to technology.
- Engage accredited technical professionals from reputable companies to help you with your digital assets.
- Educate yourself on the technology you use.

Not keeping your software current and not using virus or malware protection is akin to driving with bald tires in a blizzard. Clicking on strange or suspicious links in e-mail is no different than drinking out of a stranger's glass—you never know what you're going to catch. Using public wi-fi without encryption (i.e., not using a VPN) is akin to leaving the front and back doors of your house open all night while you are away. Digital assets are worth protecting. Invest a little time in protecting them, and it will go a long way to keeping you and your family's digital assets safe and online lives private—and therefore, more secure for the estate.

Where can one get basic computer and technical information? There are lots of online resources, news sources, educational sources, books, and magazines. Just ask your favorite techie what sources of information would be good to get you going. Check with the vendor who sold you the equipment; some vendors offer training and orientation. Be on the lookout for articles in popular magazines on protecting yourself and your family online. Some government websites offer insights on cybersecurity services and cybersecurity risks, including protecting you and your family's identity, along with protecting your devices. Given we all have busy lives, it can be difficult to find time to research, but pick one or two companies to follow on social media. You'll be surprised at how much you learn over time from following them.

Who is Managing Your Home IT Can Affect a Client's Estate

First, a shout-out to all those family members who provide technical support for their family and friends. You know who you are, because you endlessly rebuild computers and recycle equipment, so that friends and family can benefit from cool technology. You've made house calls to friends when their machine went down or printer died. You've taught their children safe internet practices, and you've tried your best to educate everyone about computing best practices. You've encouraged people to consider password managers, but you've been happy if they just wrote down their strong passwords in a small notebook they lock away when not in use (because you believe low-tech is sometimes the best tech). We've all relied on these tech wizards who patiently attend to our tech needs, who smile at us patiently when we complain that one software program doesn't work like the other, assuming they are the spokesperson for the entire technology industry. In fact, we really should have been paying for professional tech support long ago because our personal use has gone far beyond recreational.

According to the Canadian Internet Registration Authority (CIRA), 45% of Canadians say they provide informal tech support to their family and friends, and 81% of those providing support are concerned about the vulnerability of their family and friends to cyberattacks.

Advisors may want to probe to determine if their client is providing or receiving tech support from this informal community. These kinds of clients could potentially have a further need for more comprehensive plans. What if these informal support individuals get sick or are out of the country? Who is authorized to perform their tasks? Do they have a backup for those domains they manage and the network router passwords? What happens if the ersatz technical support person is out of commission? Or worse, if these individuals were providing support for a community group, volunteer organization, charity, or non-profit, what then? Business continuity planning should extend into tech and IT.

Case in Point: Windows 7 Died Without a Will

We love to stay current on tectonic shifts in technology when shiny new objects or future innovation promises to transform our paradigm or save our world.

But what about the back-office aspects of technology, namely, the maintenance side? Those oft-neglected patches, updates, privacy and security settings, backup and recovery planning—the basic tech hygiene that we rely on the IT department at work to take care of. At home, we muddle through the various tools to keep our devices operational hoping not to get an intrusion from a nefarious source who wants to infect our home device so they can "fix" it.

Let's talk about the foundation of home office technology, the operating system (OS), and how it affects estate law.

The operating system is the software that controls the operation of a computer, effectively letting users interact with their devices. Ignoring the hardcore techies and gamers for a moment, I find most home users are familiar with either Windows OS or Apple macOS, or iOS for Apple's mobile devices. Other options include Linux or Google's Chrome OS. Who hasn't been interrupted by nagging reminders from our provider to update or upgrade our OS? Usually, it's more than that. Updates are the provider's way of keeping users protected from viruses, malware, cyberintrusions, and hacking risks when new vulnerabilities are exposed.

After over 10 years of service, the Microsoft Windows 7 operating system passed away on January 14, 2020. Although the operating system will keep working, updates to protect the consumer will be no longer provided, and new software will no longer work on this version.

Operating systems don't normally get any fanfare, but Windows 7 was such a popular version that many users didn't migrate to subsequent Windows versions. As early as 2015, Microsoft offered Windows 7 users a free migration (upgrade) to Windows 10 in anticipation of the end of support, and the company strongly warned users with pop-up messages the year before it sunset.

In the months and weeks leading up to the death of Windows

7, many tech news outlets reflected fondly on the end of Windows 7 by describing its features and the reasons consumers clung to it instead of migrating to new versions.

Upgrading to a newer operating system or software application shouldn't be ignored. Users who continue to use outdated operating systems will no longer receive technical support, virus, malware, or security vulnerability protection, or software functionality updates. Some software providers do offer business and education users a degree of support for outdated software but at a cost. Apple users are also not immune to operating systems expiring.

Three reasons why estate advisors should care about the death of Windows 7:

1. For firms, companies, charities, non-profits, and businesses: Organizations stay on older versions of operating systems for a variety of reasons, including stability, cost, business impact, and concerns their applications won't work on the upgraded operating system without thorough testing. However, staying on unsupported versions of software can put the firm and their clients' data at risk in our interconnected world. Consider the Equifax data security breach that was attributed to the company not staying current on patches on their operating system.

2. Within an estate planning context and our clients' digital estates: Clients have digital assets and digital estates that need to be included in their overall estate plan. The fundamental tenet of effective estate planning of digital assets requires concerted actions on behalf of the client while they are alive because a client's data privacy and security after death can be impacted by sloppy IT hygiene during life. A client who doesn't maintain their technology risks introducing threats to their privacy and data, potentially exposing themselves to identity theft and cybercrime not only when they're alive, but after their incapacity or death. I anticipate it will be the norm for estate planners to encourage clients

to protect themselves online. Our scope should expand to include recommendations for client adherence to best practices for digital devices, digital assets, and online presence, which can include keeping hardware and software up to date. Such advice is not that different than the advice you might provide for physical assets, be they real estate or art or other collectables that typically retain value only if they are looked after, protected, and maintained.

3. Within the estate administration context: We have yet to see is how the fiduciary community will deal with an incapacitated or deceased person's device. To illustrate the point:

Suppose the will grants a fiduciary authority to deal with a deceased person's digital assets, and the deceased wished that their digital photos be provided to a family member. What if the fiduciary discovers that the deceased person's computer where the photos are stored does not have current virus protection software and the operating system is out-of-date? What should the fiduciary reasonably be expected to do in terms of time, risk, and cost? Downloading photos from the deceased's device may transfer viruses to the beneficiary's device. Or if the fiduciary attempts to update the deceased's computer, what happens if the upgraded photo software doesn't work?

Managing technology in estate administration is an emerging conversation and we've yet to see the issue to the degree described in this scenario. But just as the hackers are working on intrusions, our clients face increased risk to their digital assets.

For now, does an estate advisor need to keep up with every update for every software application? Not necessarily. An estate advisor should keep up with technology at the very least for the safety, security, and protection of their organization and as a competitive necessity for clients.

Our clients have an asset class called digital assets, and their fiduciary may encounter challenges in accessing both physical and digital assets as a result of our client's use of technology and the internet. Professional associations are taking note.

Chapter Three

Your Money, Your Memories, Your Records

Recognizing Digital Assets

Digital Asset Deep Dive: E-mail

E-mail is now the client's digital home office. It potentially contains all the information that a fiduciary would have previously found in paper statements in a home office or in an estate binder. As such, a client's e-mail may contain information about their accounts, for not only their physical assets, debts and liabilities, but all their online accounts as well. E-mail messages also likely contain valuable information about the client's relationships with the financial services and insurance institutions they deal with.

From an estate planning and estate administration perspective, a client's e-mail is a digital asset and is part of their estate and estate plan.

There are five ways our clients use e-mail that affect estate planning and eventually estate administration:

1. Clients will have wishes about who can or can't read and access their e-mail if they become incapacitated or after they have passed away. These wishes can be further complicated

by the provider's terms of service, which may deny access to others.

2. Your client's ability to transfer information and content or provide access to a fiduciary will be constrained by terms of service and the law. Two examples:

○ The Inactive Account Manager feature offered by Google's Gmail is "a way for users to share parts or all of their account data or notify someone if they've been inactive for a certain period of time." In order for the feature to work, your client will need to set it up in advance of incapacity and/or death. As it stands, if the client does not use this pre-planning function, the fiduciary will need a US court order to gain access.

○ Yahoo! Mail has no mechanism in place for a fiduciary or beneficiary to obtain access to a deceased person's e-mail account after death. The only option a fiduciary will have is to close the account.

3. E-mail accounts expire after a period of inactivity. This might not seem like an issue, but what if your client was ill prior to death and hadn't used their e-mail in a while? Microsoft's account activity policy states: "Outlook.com and OneDrive accounts will be frozen after 1 year and any e-mail messages and files stored on OneDrive will be deleted shortly after. Microsoft accounts expire after two (2) years of inactivity."

4. Clients use e-mail in a variety of intended and unintended ways that may yield surprises and risks. To illustrate: Some clients use their work e-mail to access their personal online accounts. How will that work upon death, as it is unlikely the employer will share the contents of the e-mail or the password? Some clients use e-mail to store information, such as using the draft feature or attaching documents to self-addressed e-mails. Gaining access to e-mail after death is highly restrictive for the reasons outlined above, and certainly impossible

without pre-planning. Clients should be encouraged to re-evaluate their use of e-mail as a filing system.

5. Most clients will conclude that leaving usernames and passwords for their e-mail accounts solves the problem. The problem with this approach is that the majority of online service providers' terms and conditions prevent or prohibit the use of sharing user passwords.

E-mail for Estate Planning Discovery

Here are the 10 key questions to ask your clients about e-mail for estate planning discovery:

1. What do you use e-mail for? What e-mail provider(s) do you use? How many e-mail account(s) do you have and how do you use them?

2. Who else has access to your e-mail account(s) and why? Who can reset the password on your e-mail account(s) and why?

3. Does your e-mail username(s) and profile match your given name(s)? For usernames that do not match your given name, how can you prove they are your account(s)? Are other elements of the profile accurate and up-to-date including billing information?

4. Have you reviewed the terms of service regarding what happens to your e-mail account(s) upon your death?

5. Have you used any pre-planning options offered by the e-mail provider(s)? For pre-planning functionality, do you intend to select someone other than your fiduciary? If so, why?

6. In terms of your e-mail and attachments, who do you want to be able to read or access them after death? For significant correspondence, have you saved them in another format?

7. Do you use your work e-mail for your personal online

account(s)? Have you considered changing your online account(s) to your personal e-mail versus your work e-mail?

8. Do you use your e-mail for any other purpose than communication, such as setting up online accounts? If so, have you considered exploring other more appropriate tools or software for the those purposes? For example, if your client has a draft manuscript that they send copies to themselves via e-mail for backup, have them consider using other back up methods.

9. Have you considered what information is in your e-mail that your fiduciary will need access to? Have you created a secondary source of information, such as an estate binder for your fiduciary other than expecting them to rely on e-mail? Have you also created a backup of that secondary source? How often do you plan on updating that information?

10. If it is the client's view that their e-mail is critical to their fiduciary's estate administration process, have they considered moving to an e-mail provider that provides pre-planning functions and fiduciary access? Even so, have they created a backup plan for fiduciary access to critical estate planning information?

Note, this area will evolve as consumers become more aware and demand that service providers consider these estate planning requirements. These questions are not exhaustive, and as our use of e-mail and other electronic communication evolves, these questions will change and expand. Estate planners should also seek guidance from their respective law society, estate planning professional organization, and organization's policy and practices.

Clients should be made aware of the impact that their e-mail as a digital asset has on their estate plans. They should be cautioned on solely relying on e-mail and a fiduciary's access to it as a means of transferring critical information about one's estate and estate plan. Relying on passwords is not an effective estate planning option for a variety of legal, technical, and practical reasons.

Clients should be encouraged to prepare secondary sources of information for their estate in addition to backup plans, as well as to communicate in advance with their fiduciary. The key point is that an estate plan and supporting documentation in an estate binder are as important for digital assets as they are for physical assets.

In many respects, integrating our digital lives and digital assets in estate planning also involves our clients tidying up their personal technology practices. If nothing else, they will thank you for that.

Client Management

When a client comes to you for estate planning advice with a comprehensive and detailed list of assets, the follow-on estate planning steps you should take result in developing a plan, taking client instructions, providing advice, and executing on the actions directed by the client.

What if that comprehensive list of assets the client created included a spreadsheet of every single item in their home, literally several hundred or thousands of household and personal items? You'd probably start by encouraging the client to sort these items in some meaningful way for the estate planning process. Every client's circumstances are different, but as a starting point, you might suggest that the client group items based on one or several criteria, highlight the significant item(s), or ask the client if they want the entire lot dealt with in the same way.

The client management approach is similar, if not the same, for digital assets.

Although a password manager, a program allowing users to store, generate, and manage passwords for online services, offers a convenient starting point as an inventory, it won't tell you all the things you need to know to properly advise the client. In all likelihood, other than the purely virtual assets, such as unregulated cryptocurrencies, social media accounts, or data in the cloud, you'll likely find the majority of the items on a client's digital asset list are underlying assets or contractual relationships, accessed online through a virtual gateway. Examples include online access to financial institutions, household utility bills, and other liabilities. You will also want to understand the significant items and the more complex assets that are intertwined with financial institutions, as well as management considerations for digital photos, music scores or song lyrics, or manuscripts where copyrights are involved.

Digital Asset Planning Guidance

In addition to reviewing your organization's estate planning processes for digital asset guidance, you should encourage clients to do the following:

- Create a digital assets inventory as part of their estate inventory. As with key physical assets, the client should highlight the digital assets of financial and sentimental value.

- Include a jurisdiction-specific digital assets clauses in their will, power of attorney, and trust agreements.

- Keep their digital assets inventory up to date and to not include passwords. Their updates should include any technical management instructions and appropriate access instructions in light of legal and other constraints. As other pre-planning options become available, they will need to be examined to ensure they do not conflict with the powers given to the fiduciary or instructions provided in other legal documents.

- Keep an estate binder. At the very least it should include a list of all assets — physical and digital. With everyone moving to online statements and accounts to manage their underlying assets, it will be important for the fiduciary to know what holdings the client has and at what institution.

- Talk with their fiduciary. With no paper trail and the increasing number and complexity of assets that the average person now owns, it will not be obvious where one should start. How to handle digital assets is a new conversation required between the client and their fiduciary.

Rely on the Basics

It is perfectly reasonable to rely on your estate planning basics when asking questions about digital assets.

Here is a starting set of questions that you can ask your client. Consider the following:

- What are the most important digital assets you own?
- Have you left enough information for the fiduciary to contact companies directly to close down your subscription services?
- Have you reviewed the terms of service?
- Have you used pre-planning tools, if provided?
- Have you created detailed instructions for the fiduciary?
- Have you tested those instructions?

As this area evolves and the law progresses, and as service providers begin to respond to pressure, we may see more mainstream solutions to address estate planning and estate administration of digital assets. Even so, your core competency remains the same: ferreting out the important, doing the research, and providing advice for specific assets in estate planning, but now with a digital twist.

The Dangers of Ignoring E-mail

In today's court of public opinion, amplified by social media, estate planners should expect clients and their beneficiaries to express their displeasure if not advised of the impact digital assets as simple as e-mail could have on estate planning.

E-mail is the foundation of the new home office and gateway to your client's information. Without pre-planning, the fiduciary may end up dead-in-the-water without access to the critical information needed to find even physical assets, let alone maximizing the value of the client's estate.

Not all digital assets are the same.

In some cases, they share the same characteristics as physical assets and rights, but they can also have unique characteristics with dramatic differences within a similar type of digital asset. What predominately drives these differences are the service provider offerings, and their terms of service.

Unlike earlier digital eras, we are in new territory where many of our online accounts are free to use. We are using accounts in ways even the original service providers hadn't imagined with client use of digital assets varying widely, and legal precedents only beginning to emerge.

Legal precedent in the estate planning and estate administration space is new and evolving and how a client uses a particular digital asset can vary widely.

This myriad of client uses of digital assets and their peculiarities pose challenges for estate planners and lawyers who need to get under the covers of common digital asset characteristics in order to more effectively advise clients. Fundamentally, digital assets impact two aspects of the estate planning process, but it all begins with disclosure.

First, digital assets need to be part of the normal estate planning process and covered during disclosure, analysis, client goal documentation, and options, risks, and instrument identification.

Second, the technology itself will have unique handling instructions due to the client's use of the technology; whether the technology offers pre-planning options and whether there are any barriers-on-transfer due to incapacity and death could impede timely estate closure.

How E-mail Is Really Used
E-mail is a form of communication, an electronic replacement for paper letters between parties. In reality, our modern use of e-mail

is much more than that, and our clients spend a great deal of their time on e-mail and other platforms, at both home and work. We also use e-mail in ways that the inventors couldn't possibly have imagined. For many, it has become a digital repository of records, information, and calendar entries, and a link to their entire lives.

The lines have blurred between pure correspondence exchange with e-mail and information transfer with social media accounts, shared calendars, contact lists, apps, other platform-specific features, accounts on the cloud, and single sign-on, allowing cross-platform integration. Our e-mail address is no longer simply representative of a mailbox, it also serves as the log-in credential or username for other applications and online services.

Where Is All This E-mail Coming From?

Clients use a myriad of personal e-mail options depending on any number of circumstances. As CNBC reported in 2019, Google's Gmail is certainly a predominate player with 1.5 billion users globally; others include Microsoft's Outlook, and Yahoo! Mail. Clients also use e-mail bundled with other services from providers. The e-mail options are endless—from hosted domains to family domains to other providers, including work, school, or volunteer organizations.

Digital Assets Deep Dive: Tech Solutions

At many workshops and conferences, I have spoken with estate advisors, estate planners, clients, and the general public. Regardless of the audience, some of the first words often blurted out are "password managers" (or in the form of a question, "What about password managers?"), in an effort to handily solve the entire digital assets dilemma in one fell swoop.

We live in a complicated world where every minute of the day is taken up by client commitments, and we don't have the time to investigate a new and evolving digital domain that requires more research than can be covered by a passing comment.

Hard copy lists of passwords and online password managers

offer only a technical solution to manage long and complex passwords in our digital inventory. Transferring digital assets upon death is complicated by legal, technical, and practical challenges inherent in the contractual relationship we have with our online providers outlined in their terms of service.

The law is still evolving, and the business and technological options for pre-planning are immature. Though there are recognized solutions, such as Facebook's Legacy Contact and Google's Inactive Account Manager, pre-planning options are mostly nonexistent.

Starting Point in Discovery

From an estate planning perspective, information from a password manager, provided it is extracted as a list of usernames, service providers, and websites, may be a starting point in discovery. But it won't do the following:

- Identify or verify a client's key assets.
- Tell you the terms of service.
- Answer questions about ownership rights.
- Include the client's goals, wishes, and preferences.
- Identify risks.
- Provide detailed instructions on how to manage the assets from a technology perspective.
- Offer recommended strategies for dealing with a client's requirements.

And more concerning, a locked and encrypted vault of any type, including a password manager, will pose unique access challenges for the fiduciary. Regardless of what the law and the contractual terms of service dictate, what if the password for the password manager was noted incorrectly or not updated, or required secondary authentication, or had other access barriers? What if your client was ill for a long time before they died and stopped paying the credit card for the password manager subscription service?

Technological Solutions Compound the Problem

It's easy to jump to a technological solution as the be-all-and-end-all to our business problems.

As those involved in developing or maintaining client systems know very well, solution development starts with defining the business problem. Invariably the best technical solutions, even those right out of the box, generally come with an equal if not larger business process engineering requirement.

For successful solution implementation, the client must evaluate what they are doing and why, along with the education, change management, communication, and maintenance requirements as new systems often result in additional, unexpected requirements, with time needed to work out the kinks. Rarely have I seen a successful technology project where the technical solution stood on its own without inordinate effort before and after its implementation with an integrated effort between business owners and the service providers.

Reframing the Question

In that vein, let's reframe the question of how best to manage digital assets. If we don our estate planning hats and turn to a business process answer as a starting point for handling digital assets, we, as experienced planners, should leverage the processes and practices we already know.

Then the questions become, How does a client plan for their digital assets after death, and is a password manager part of the equation?

Take the hypothetical situation of a client who comes to you for estate planning advice with a comprehensive and detailed list of assets—personal and business interests, a family tree, and a list of preferences. You'd probably be delighted as it would aid the assessment or discovery phase of your information-gathering process, but it's the follow-on steps and executing the actions directed by the client that are critical.

Digital Assets Deep Dive: Social Media

Data Privacy in Death Begins by Managing Data Privacy in Life

Social media is not immune to death with its own form of either digital death or a digital legacy.

In 2019, there was a surge in media outlets reporting on the growing number of deceased persons on Facebook and that they could potentially outnumber the living—and this was before the COVID-19 pandemic. Twitter had its own estate planning challenges in late 2019 when the company announced that it would close inactive accounts after six months.

The death-positive movement on social media protested, and stories of how this policy would affect survivors of deceased persons fueled the tweet storm. Shortly thereafter, Twitter responded by saying it would not remove inactive accounts and would look at implementing a memorialization feature.

From an estate planning perspective, the number of deceased persons on social media may not seem like a relevant estate planning concern, but how our clients use social media can dramatically affect their overall estate from a privacy, financial, and sentimental value perspective.

Without documented instructions for actions upon incapacity or death, there could be a significant mismatch in expectations between the intentions of the account owner and their fiduciary, and potentially between the family and the beneficiaries regarding how to deal with the deceased's social media presence or access to digital assets. All of which could be further constrained by the law and the social media provider's terms of service. As we know for physical assets, a lack of documented wishes can lead to conflict, time delays, and even estate litigation before the fiduciary can sort out the estate administration path forward.

A Starting Point in Discovery

Social media is truly a product of the information age although its historical roots are said to date back to the introduction of the telegraph. According to Wikipedia, there are 13 types of social media communities ranging from blogs, photo sharing, social networks, and enterprise networks to social gaming. Most people refer to social media by the name of the social platform or provider they use most often, such as LinkedIn, Facebook, Twitter, or Pinterest.

The use of social media for sharing information, posting photos, and communicating among friends and family or even within a community is mainstream. According to *Forbes*, of the top ten most downloaded social and messaging apps in 2019, Facebook Inc. owns four of them: Facebook, Instagram, Messenger, and WhatsApp.

Not as obvious in the social media category are gaming apps or sites (e.g., Minecraft, World of Warcraft, The Elder Scrolls Online, Black Desert Online, Blizzard, Fortnite), with some of these known as *massively multiplayer online role-playing games* (MMORPG), where players engage, transact, compete, and communicate in a virtual world.

Technological Solutions Compound the Problem

As mainstream and integrated into our daily lives as social media seems to be, so eventually will be our client's wishes regarding their social media accounts upon incapacity or death. The term to describe these expectations is *digital legacy*. The idea is that our clients interact online creating a digital presence or leaving a digital footprint that will need to be addressed in estate planning. James Norris of the Digital Legacy Association offers a conversational definition of digital legacy: *"Our digital legacy is what remains of us digitally once we die. When we die our digital footprint becomes our digital legacy."*

Our engagement in the digital age, be it with a new class of assets called digital assets or even the modern-day obituary, needs a rethink for privacy, the risk of identity theft, and cyberintrusion.

Unlike a physical asset or rights, it is not simply a matter of the fiduciary freezing an account or changing the locks for an online account such as a social media account. Our digital tidiness and information technology habits while we are living influence the risk profile of both our physical and digital estates upon death.

Terms of use, terms of service, or provider contracts control what a fiduciary can and can't do upon the death of the account owner. The master of all disguises are the evolving terms of service where online providers often reserve the right to update or change the terms at any point. There just may not be the certainty that a specific online service or function offered by a provider will continue indefinitely, particularly when you consider most social media platforms offer free access for basic service.

Reframing the Question

As with any online account, an individual's use of social media and their preferences for incapacity and death will depend on exactly what they are using the social platform for and how they use it while they are living.

The complexity for estate planners increases for the following reasons:

- Clients will have wishes regarding their social media online presence upon incapacity and/or death. Without guidance, families, beneficiaries, and fiduciaries may have preferences that may differ from those of the testator (will-maker). The challenge, as with all estate planning, is that the client's specific wishes for their social media and digital legacies will be as individual as the person themselves, and may differ between different types of digital assets, or even between social media accounts within the same class. A client may want their family to have access to their photos on a social media platform but may want other social media accounts closed after death or upon incapacity. For a psychological perspective of social media and digital legacy wishes, see Dr. Elaine Kasket's book *All the Ghosts in the Machine: The Digital Afterlife of Your Personal Data*. Through interviews and cases, author and psychologist Dr. Kasket outlines the spectrum of differing wishes of the testator (will-maker) and the beneficiaries, family, or fiduciary, and the challenges of meeting those wishes in our current context of the law and service provider terms of service. Dr. Kasket also explores how the ways we grieve are changing as a result of our use of social media and technology. She further cautions against relying on social media platforms to store memories.

- Clients may have monetized their use of social platforms or use them in ways that retain forms of financial or other exchange-able value. A client may be using a social media account that generates revenue, has brand or financial value, or is collect-ing tokens that have some form of value. One example is a client receiving ad revenue for posting content. Even gaming platforms have a form of currency where value is exchanged between players, or value is retained in virtual constructs (tools, costumes, avatars, rewards, weapons, levels) that are bought and sold, awarded or won on the platform.

- Data privacy upon incapacity and/or death is affected by life. In an internet-connected world, users are providing significantly more information online globally than ever. Social media envi-ronments lend themselves to our providing excessive informa-tion, including personal information about where we live, our relationships, our workplace, our vacations, our possessions, and our opinions.

  ○ I recall a social media post—visible to the world, from an elated young woman who had received gifts from her three children. They had framed their artwork in celebration of her birthday, and in the picture the full legal name and birth-day of each of the children was proudly captioned beneath their respective artwork.

  ○ Facebook allows users to configure their privacy setting while the account owner is alive, allowing them to control who sees what content. There is a difference between public access, where anyone can see anything, to restricted access where only friends can see the posted content. An account owner can set privacy settings while alive, but after death, even if the account owner appointed a Legacy Contact, the privacy settings can never be modified. In simple terms, if an account is public while the account owner is alive, it will remain public after death. That in itself may be an estate planning concern if the testator wishes for the fiduciary to lock down the privacy settings or remove content of the account after death. As per Facebook's policy Managing Deceased Person's Account: "Depending on the privacy settings of the account, friends can share memories on the memorialized timeline."

- Some social media platforms offer pre-planning options, but they need to be activated while the account owner is alive. Pre-planning functions are not the norm in most online accounts. These examples are illustrative of service provider differences at a point in time. Check the current terms of services for the service providers you use:

  ○ Facebook has created three pre-planning options. The account owner can: (1) have their account memorialized or permanently deleted upon their death, (2) identify a Legacy Contact, and (3) opt for the tribute feature released in 2019.
  ○ Instagram has a memorialization function with different features than Facebook. Instagram allows "verified immediate family members" with proof to memorialize the account or remove the account of a deceased person.
  ○ LinkedIn does not currently have pre-planning functions. It does allow any member to report a deceased member, and it also allows someone "authorized to act on behalf of a deceased member" to memorialize or close the member's account.
  ○ Twitter does not currently have pre-planning functions. It does allow others to request a deceased or incapacitated person's account to be deactivated.

- The available pre-planning functions are a lot more restrictive than you would think in terms of estate planning options. Unless there is emerging consumer consultation, and collaboration between regulatory bodies and industry, I think we will continue to see disparately different and limited options. It has yet to be seen if providers will offer pre-planning options distinguishing incapacity from death. How long a provider will be around and what obligations they feel they need to provide have yet to be seen. They do retain the right to change their terms of service. Here are some examples of the limitations:

  ○ Facebook has three pre-planning choices outlined above. Within the Legacy Contact option, the Legacy Contact's permissions are outlined in the Help section: a Legacy Contact can't read messages, make friend requests, or change content in the timeline. And the Legacy Contact must have a Facebook account.

  ○ Facebook's feature for reporting incapacity allows for only one option: a request for the removal of an account if the owner is medically incapacitated.

  ○ Google's pre-planning feature, Inactive Account Manager, allows users to select an individual who will be notified of inactivity or the sharing of account data. While it addresses incapacity to a degree, it monitors only inactivity—whether as a result of incapacity, death, or simply infrequent use. After months of inactivity, Google indicates they would consider the account inactive but will contact the user before any action is taken. For a fiduciary who may need immediate access to information about an incapacitated or deceased person, months can be a lifetime—assuming the fiduciary was the person selected to be notified.

- The client may be using a social platform beyond what it was intended for or could have unrealistic expectations about what happens to content after incapacity or death. If a client set up a social media account to blog on a specific hobby, but the hobby evolves into a business, any plans for access after death need to be established in advance.

Case in Point: Protecting Clients' Wishes and Privacy in Life and in Death

Discussion about a client's e-mail or loyalty points has not traditionally been part of an estate lawyer's conversation with the testator (will-maker). But in the digital age, the client's ever-expanding digital estate, including social media, should be part of the estate planning conversation. Given the expanse of different social media platform types and choices within a type, the questions during discovery could be endless, depending on how frequently the client uses social media.

Consider these deep-dive considerations to explore your client's technology use across different platforms:

- Encourage clients to create an estate inventory including digital assets, in addition to planning their will and engaging in other estate planning activities. Have them update the inventory regularly. The STEP Inventory was provided as an example earlier. Details to include:
  - Websites for online accounts and usernames (which may differ from their legal names).
  - Information that ties an account owner to a specific username. There may be platforms where there is no other personal authenticating information such as a credit card or a full legal name.
  - Information regarding where backups are stored.
  - Where backups can be retrieved, and noting the instructions for each account, as recommended by the Digital Legacy Association.
- Without pre-planning and guidance, a social media account is likely to remain active long after the death of the account owner (unless the provider has a terms of use policy for

inactive accounts). Questions to ask the account owner about each social media account:

- ○ Upon their death, do they want the account to remain online (memorialized, if available) or deactivated, noting a client may have different choices for each account? One wish for their professional social media accounts and another for their dating site accounts?
- ○ Upon their incapacity, what are their preferences, even though the pre-planning options available may limit their choices?

- Encourage clients to use pre-planning functions if they are available but understand their limitations. If this function exists, it would be found in settings or via a quick search in the help center. For example:

  - ○ A client may use a social media account to research legacy information, such as genealogy. Some genealogy accounts allow others to set up their own profile and obtain access to information from the original account owner. These options must be set up while the account owner is alive.

- 4. Some clients may monetize their social media use or use them in a way that has financial or other convertible value. Key questions:

  - ○ Does the client have a social media account that is generating revenue or has brand or financial value?
  - ○ Are they receiving revenue for posting content?
  - ○ Have they left instructions on how the fiduciary can legally access these accounts and what is required for estate administration?
  - ○ Have legal instructions been drafted that address wishes about these accounts?
  - ○ Which assets can be transferred in advance of incapacity or death and under what circumstances?
  - ○ For their personal accounts, ask if their social media

account can be converted to a business account or adjunct page, where others such as the fiduciary can be added with administrative privileges?

- Review the privacy settings of online accounts on a regular basis. Encourage clients to have private or restricted accounts rather than public accounts. Clients should consider separate social media accounts for various audiences. It is not uncommon to have a client start with a personal page that evolves to include business clients or interests. Having separate accounts or pages allows a client to more tightly manage access, privacy, and content specific to an audience. A client may want a business page open to the public, but a client page restricted to current clients and a personal account that is only for friends and family.

- Some social media providers offer business accounts or pages separate from a personal account or profile. Typically, these business accounts allow individual(s) who are granted access to manage the page or have other access privileges. This is a powerful tool to manage access of multiple person(s) to a page and is useful in estate planning when transferring ownership or management of a page to others.

- If a client's social media content is important to them, they should back it up regularly or provide a secondary source of access to what is stored on these platforms. Consider:
  - Many clients use social media to share photos, but those platforms may be the only place where they have stored those photos.
  - Social media platforms often offer functions that allow users to download their data.
  - With the current limitations for pre-planning on many social media platforms, the Digital Legacy Association offers free public social media guides on its "For the Public" page where the association recommends downloading important information regularly.

- If clients predominately use social media to share photos with friends and family, they should consider making those files accessible on other shared drives or hard copy print outs.

- The client may have created or be part of a community, group, forum, or blog that has intrinsic value, that either the account owner or the community itself will want to continue after the incapacity and/or death of the testator. This arrangement is similar to members of a lottery pool who document rules of engagement. Consider:

  - Use of platforms that support secondary or business pages, allowing access to others, with regular data backup on a secondary source.
  - Document community or group agreements among member owners or administrators to include:
  - What is expected in terms of access.
  - Departure of members.
  - Death or incapacity of administrators or owners.
  - Continuity or longevity of the group.
  - Backup and recovery of the blog, forum, or site.

- The client's social media content may also be tied to physical property rights or intellectual property rights.

  - Has the client left detailed instruction on how the fiduciary is to access the content?
  - What is required to facilitate estate administration?
  - Have appropriate legal instructions and directives been drafted to address client wishes about these assets?
  - Which assets can be transferred in advance of incapacity and death and under what circumstances?
  - Can personal social media accounts be converted to business accounts where additional members with administrative privileges can be added, with appropriate legalities followed?

Rely on the Basics

This space is evolving. Given the overall limitations and lack of mainstream pre-planning tools for online accounts, advise clients to do the following:

- Establish their privacy settings while they are alive.
- Purge accounts and content that is no longer of use.
- Use any pre-planning functions that are available.
- Regularly download and back up any data (such as photos) they want someone to have access to after their incapacity and/or death.

Chapter Four

Today's Executor is a Digital Executor

Technology is the new player at your client's estate planning table, making the future executor a digital executor. The future is here.

One of the effects of the pandemic is that it has immersed many of your clients in technology. Forced to shift non-essential work to remote work and now reliant on technology to keep their social connections, your clients are likely dependent on tech like never before.

Technology immersion includes the gamut of videoconferencing for work meetings, Zoom for fitness classes, online grocery shopping, online banking, and the internet as a sandbox for new hobbies. Our world has a whole new vocabulary driven by digital immersion. Terms such as Zoombombing, telemedicine, flattening the curve, and contact tracing have entered the everyday lexicon. Your client may not have had a digital life, digital assets, or a digital estate before the pandemic, but they do now. And this digital existence has an implication on estate planning, incapacity planning, and estate administration.

As discussed, STEP considers digital assets to have some of the same characteristics as physical assets, such as having financial or sentimental value.

***There are three questions about digital assets
the modern-day fiduciary and advisors should ask:***

1. How will clients and their beneficiaries feel if digital assets are lost? Just as you would advise a client on planning for their prized physical possessions, the same must be said for their digital assets. For digital assets of sentimental value, such as social media accounts, preferences about account memorialization might be just as important to the deceased as to what happens to their beloved pet or coin collection.

2. Is the executor, estate trustee, or fiduciary ready? As I've argued, without the client leaving a paper trail, the amount of lost or inaccessible assets (both physical and digital) will grow, challenging estate administration. There is also the issue of volume. It's not uncommon for people to have close to a hundred online accounts, and just as likely, clients may have their physical lives intertwined with their digital lives.

The fiduciary will need to work at digital speed. No longer a matter of when they will get around to changing the physical locks on the deceased's home, the fiduciary will need to immediately lock down the deceased's digital life to prevent identity theft. Social media may seem trivial and the last thing a family needs to worry about at the time of death of a loved one, but social media provides a wealth of information for cyberthieves upon the client's incapacity and/or death, which should be of material concern for the fiduciary.

Corporate fiduciaries and trust companies are only now beginning to realize the implications of their client's digital assets, but they haven't yet raised a collective alarm bell. Arguably, the average age of today's trust company client needing administration mutes the growing swell of clients with extensive digital portfolios.

3. Are the client's digital assets accessible? If clients do not plan for their digital assets, those assets will likely be invisible, inaccessible, or not transferable upon incapacity and death. In this new world, including technical management considerations will be required in an estate plan in addition to the more traditional estate planning constructs. Documenting, testing, and communicating tech management plans are now considered essential, but estate advisors and clients may need to engage technical advisors or technologists with specialties to support their planning processes.

Provider terms of service (TOS), situs of a client's digital assets, and jurisdiction-specific fiduciary access laws will significantly hamper planning efforts.

Looking ahead: If technology is the new player at your client's estate planning table, then the estate advisory community, including corporate fiduciaries and trustees, need to be not only tech ready and knowledgeable, but capable of guiding clients through this new planning paradigm.

Specifically, the entire client engagement life cycle and the associated risk management framework, needs to be updated to address digital assets. Organizations and non-profits need to consider the platforms and tools involved and deal with the volume and variance of a client's digital portfolio in planning and administration. Fiduciaries must be knowledgeable about technology and this new asset class, comfortable with the subject when engaging with clients during planning and remain current as technology changes.

Digital Assets Planning Myths

Planning for digital assets is not a new topic. Estate planners have been discussing this topic for the last 10 years, and yet during this time of rapid global technology adoption, the topic of digital assets remains one of the least understood aspects of estate planning and estate administration.

From a technology management perspective, I've seen no less than three myths circulating on how to handle this new asset class in estate planning. There is the misunderstanding that all digital assets are the same, password managers and hard copy password lists are the answer, and the appointment of a digital asset fiduciary solves the problem.

Myth #1: All Digital Assets Are the Same

In 2017, the value of Bitcoin rose, increasing public awareness of unregulated cryptocurrencies and leading to revisiting the conversation on the financial implications of owning cryptoassets. Are these digital assets handled the same way as an e-mail account? Would you handle a client's fine art collection the same way as their real-estate holdings?

While the volume of digital assets in estate administration grows, until corporate fiduciaries and trust companies start raising alarm bells, unfortunately, we may continue to see these myths perpetuate.

Digital assets have been described as unique assets and grouped in the same asset class along with the art collection, rare sculptures, or other historically significant artifacts.

The definition of a digital asset I shared earlier, as simply an electronic record, can make it seem innocuous and uniform. Compare digital assets with physical objects that are mostly made up of water: each physical object is characteristically different that we may not even know it contains water. Digital assets are likewise vastly different.

The STEP definition offers more nuance, as the Society recognizes that digital assets may have financial or sentimental value. This definition is a useful conversation starter with clients because it draws in all the other more familiar process steps in estate planning. Consider listing digital assets along with other assets and client wishes, providing equal weight and importance. The conversation should also consider any tax liabilities associated with these assets.

Digital assets are not all the same and estate advisors should treat each one as having unique value to that particular client. Some digital assets, such as online access to financial institutions, are governed by rules set by the financial institution. So much so, that fiduciaries should not be accessing these digital assets and should be dealing directly with the institution to establish their own access, if required, supported by the legal documentation the individual holds. Even within types of digital assets, such as e-mail or loyalty points, what is allowed upon death will differ within each provider's terms of service.

To address the myth that all digital assets are the same, I recommend estate advisors ask their clients to identify their top three digital assets. Then I suggest asking the individual how devastated they would be if the assets were not transferred. Those assets could be e-mail correspondence, loyalty points, their wishes for online memorialization, or the handling of unregulated cryptocurrencies. Review the distinguishing features of each asset, considering the terms of service or technical management characteristics of each. Most importantly, develop an estate plan addressing the unique aspects of each digital asset, so they can be effectively managed upon incapacity and transferred upon death.

A client's e-mail account is as significant in estate administration as it is in today's home office. Clients should be urged to create an estate inventory or list of all their significant assets—physical and digital, as a fiduciary can no longer rely on a paper trail. It's unwise to rely solely on the fiduciary's ability to gain access to a client's e-mail account because there is a high degree of risk the fiduciary will be unable to do so.

Myth #2: Password Managers and Hard Copy Lists Are the Answer

Sharing passwords might seem like a convenient answer to the problem of transferring digital assets, but it is a superficial solution for a variety of legal, technical, and practical reasons.

The biggest barrier is the terms of service imposed by service providers, which may prevent the account owner from sharing the password(s). A fiduciary could be exposed to legal liability by attempting to access an account after death, even if the individual they are acting on behalf of has given them their passwords.

From a technical perspective, all the barriers imposed to protect users from cybercrime will be the same barriers the fiduciary is confronted with. It may not be technically possible to use someone's password even if you were allowed to do so legally. Passwords change over time, passwords get written down incorrectly, and users are often required to perform a two-step verification through text message. What if the cell phone was cut off because the credit card was frozen, and there was no longer a secondary method available?

Relying on passwords to transfer valuable digital assets is ineffective and precarious. Password managers are for the living. With the proliferating number of online accounts the average person has, password managers can be useful for storing unique and complex passwords as we strive for cybersecurity; however, other pre-planning options are required for the estate planning of digital assets.

According to the study "Beyond the Clouds" from the Cloud Legal Project at Queen Mary University of London, more than 85% of cloud providers do not have terms that address incapacity and/ or death of the account owners. This means your fiduciary might get frustrated dealing with customer support trying to get access to your account even with the correct documentation.

There are certainly emerging tech entrepreneurs offering digital vaults to manage our tech, as well as solutions to document directives on dealing with providers.

I believe we will need the same spectrum of estate planning choices for digital assets as we have for physical assets, such as insurance, beneficiary designations, joint ownership, and pre-planning and transfer options. Quite concerned about the lack of consumer options, I co-authored an article with US attorney Jennifer Zegel for Bloomberg Tax Insight called "Supporting Your Clients' Digital Legacy." This article explored the options and other pre-planning considerations that service providers and, in fact, all online businesses should be considering. I've been saying for a while that we need the same spectrum of choices in estate planning for our digital assets as we have for our physical assets, and right now there are not a lot of pre-planning options. I believe this is due to the lack of awareness by consumers, and therefore has not yet translated into a marketplace demand.

There is really no such thing as joint ownership of an online account, but maybe there should be. It is unlikely that a variety of options will appear in the near term, as it will take time for consumers to become aware of the issue and demand more choice from providers. For now, all we can do is encourage clients to use the pre-planning options that are available and seek legal advice. For significant digital assets, encourage clients to explore using business accounts instead of personal accounts, as business accounts often provide multiple user access.

Myth #3: Appointing a Digital Executor Solves the Problem

As I previously outlined, *digital executor* is a made-up term. It sounds convenient, but this myth is likely based on an oversimplification of the digital asset class conversation and a lack of recognizing how intertwined our digital lives are with our physical lives. Unfortunately, there are a myriad of other titles emerging to describe this person who is separate from the fiduciary.

When your client has a subscription to an online newspaper, magazine, or streaming service and engages with that platform through their browser, who is supposed to deal with this digital asset— the executor or the digital executor?

Now consider the flipside. Suppose your client has an unregulated cryptocurrency and specialized technical help may be required to deal with this asset. But what about the taxes? Does the digital executor of the fiduciary deal with the tax liability?

From a project management perspective, what is happening is that today's fiduciary has to deal with not only traditional estate matters, but also the deceased's digital estate. Additionally, there are jurisdiction-specific laws that govern what a fiduciary, or anyone for that matter, can and can't do in handling a client's digital life, digital assets, and online accounts.

Just as fiduciaries engage specialists depending on the asset, such as an art appraiser for art, or a real estate agent for property, in the digital age, the fiduciary may need specialized advice in dealing with the client's digital life. Providing the fiduciary with powers in a client's will and other estate planning instruments to deal with their digital assets and digital estate is a good starting point. Identifying additional guidance or technical support that the fiduciary may need is another worthy measure.

Consider these findings from the Cloud Legal Project survey on TOS contracts:

- Users are generally not permitted to assign their rights under cloud contracts.
- The TOS of most cloud services do not address what happens when a user dies.
- The TOS of all cloud services surveyed prohibited user password sharing.
- The TOS of around one-third of cloud service providers surveyed stipulated that user accounts would be terminated upon inactivity.
- Cloud providers can typically change their TOS after notifying users of any material changes, either by e-mail or through the service.

Given how dependent we are on technology, and the power of the digital custodians, I expect once consumers have heightened awareness, they will demand better options for estate planning from service providers.

The unfortunate reality is that digital assets are difficult to access after death. This notion of a digital estate has emerged only in the past 30 years as a result of our reliance on the internet. It's critical we raise our client's awareness of their digital assets and the impact they have on their estate plans.

Help educate your clients and your colleagues by busting these three myths about digital assets in estate planning. I'm sure as the topic evolves, we'll continue to see other myths. If you are looking for further digital planning myths, check out the Bloomberg Tax Insight article I co-authored with Jennifer Zegel. This article, called "Five Signs That Estate Advisors Aren't Getting With the Digital Program", covers five more red flags:

1. When an estate advisor says a will is enough to handle your digital life and digital assets, or that a will insert is enough to handle your digital life and digital assets.
2. When your estate advisor swims outside their lane and gives you technical advice. An estate advisor should likely seek expert technical advice.)
3. When your estate advisor tells you all you need to do is leave passwords and magically all your digital assets will be taken care of after your death. Know the limitations of passwords and password managers.
4. When your estate planner tells you to let your family sort out your social media.
5. When your advisor throws around invented terminology.

Rethinking Obituaries in the Digital Age

A Starting Point in Discovery

We're told not to click on links in e-mails, not to open attachments from unknown sources, and not to provide personal information to someone we don't know on the phone or online. So why is it we still create obituaries, also known as death notices, as if we are completing a job application, regardless if it is a legal declaration or memorial announcement? It seems writers make sure every inordinate fact and figure is accurate, spelled correctly, and packed with personal detail down to the size of gym shorts worn in high school. I've seen a boatload of information shoved into every sentence of an obituary exposing much more than just information on the deceased: details on entire families are included, from the names of children, grandchildren, and partners to pets.

In the digital age, the modern-day obituary needs a rethink

for privacy, identity theft risk, and cyberintrusion of not only the deceased, but also those whose personal information has been inadvertently released. Cybercrime and the use of social engineering to perpetrate fraud doesn't just happen with the obvious information such as names and birthdates; identity theft can also happen with secondary pieces of information, such as university degrees, places of residence, and the names of employers.

Reframing the Requirement

If we think of obituary surfing as a crime of opportunity, perhaps we need to rethink its purpose and place in the digital age. According to the *Online Etymology Dictionary*, the obituary as we know it dates back to 1738. Today, the obituary serves the same purpose as a record or announcement of a death. But death notices have mushroomed from fewer than 50 words in the mid-twentieth century to 500-word essays. It's worth asking why the lengthy obituary is the norm, particularly when it brings so much risk. Is it simply a result of our sharing obsession, or is it part of the grieving process? Shorter obituaries will likely frustrate genealogists but consider the flip side and how much information is available already on social platforms. The point is, the obituary is for the living and is a valuable tool to communicate information about an individual's passing and memorialization, but it is also an opportunity for information theft.

Technological Solutions Compound the Obituary Problem

Why does personal information in an obituary suddenly appear to be an issue in the digital age? Historically, an obituary was printed in the local paper, readily available only to those who lived within the circulation route of the particular edition of that paper. Certainly, when newspaper archives moved to microfiche storage, this historical information became more widely available, but in the digital age, the newspaper is available not only in print, but also digitally from anywhere in the world. Furthermore, many newspaper outlets offer not only the announcement in a print edition, but an online memorial that is accessible for months or years. It doesn't stop there. Memorialization, whether we have planned it or not, has moved into the social media realm where anyone, can write anything about anyone. And here's another risk to consider: detailed information about a deceased's partner or spouse in an obituary can leave the surviving member of the couple vulnerable and a target for bad actions down the road. Police and government agencies have begun to warn the public about sharing personal information in obituaries.

Planning Guidance and What to Do to Better Protect Your Client's Privacy in Life and in Death

Discussion about the client's e-mail, and obituary for that matter, has not traditionally been part of an estate lawyer's conversation with the testator (will-maker). But in the digital age, not only should digital assets and the client's ever-expanding digital estate be part of the conversation, but so should a risk assessment of the role of the fiduciary. In other words, is the fiduciary up to the task of handling the digital estate?

Encourage the client to talk with their fiduciary about their obituary or written memorial wishes—in terms of not only how the person wants to be remembered, but also, more importantly in the digital age, which personal information should be included.

Several directives for consideration:

- Review any legal requirement for notifications upon death, for creditors or otherwise. Discuss with the client and their fiduciary what is the minimum information required for any legal notifications.

- Review the need for the traditional newspaper or organizational alumni obituary at all. If the client still has wishes for an obituary or memorial notice, advise the client and their fiduciary to eliminate or reduce the amount of personally identifiable information in the obituary.

  ○ Do not provide a birthdate. Do not be precise with the

death date. Eliminate the date and month, and use the year sparingly, round to "x year young," or consider if this information is necessary.

- ○ Do not provide the deceased's full legal name. Consider using a common name or nickname versus a full legal name. Delete the middle name, delete other names (also known as), and rethink the need to include maiden names.
- ○ Eliminate the names of family members, referring to loved ones by role instead: "The deceased is survived by their loving spouse, 6 children, and 12 grandchildren."
- ○ Eliminate names of cities, schools, degrees, and any other specific pieces of information that can be used for identity theft or for fraud by social engineering.
- ○ Avoid any chronology of personal or work history that includes specific names, dates, and locations.
- ○ Avoid providing specific information (e.g., date, address) about the funeral or celebration of life event. Provide a channel for attendees to obtain information that is not public.

- Discuss other options and what you can include instead. Focus on the attributes, contribution, and character of the deceased, and stories about them—information that is unique and memorable but cannot be compromised.

- Encourage your client to discuss their memorialization preferences for their social media and public platforms with their fiduciary. Do they want their accounts to remain online, memorialized, or removed? As very few providers offer pre-planning options other than deactivating an account, I expect this to change in the coming years. For example, if your client has a Facebook profile, they should consider memorializing their account and selecting a Legacy Contact if they want tribute posts or continued account management after their death; otherwise, the client can opt to have their account deleted after their death. Recommend that your client adjust the privacy settings of their social media accounts while they are alive, in addition to selecting pre-planning options as they become available. If the client plans on choosing a legacy contact other than the fiduciary, you should inquire why.

- Encourage your client to consider other memorial and notification options. There are an emerging number of tech entrepreneurs offering options to leave messages to specific loved ones versus public announcements after death.

- Encourage clients to close accounts they don't use and check the privacy settings on all their online accounts. A concerning privacy risk not only in life but also upon death is a poorly protected account where anyone in the world, with the simple press of a button or click of a mouse, can see your profile or comment on your timeline. Potentially, an unsecured profile alerts cybercriminals, and they may just hear about your client's passing before the important people in the client's life.

- Among the many ways that a fiduciary could secure a deceased person's life, including securing assets and informing government agencies (e.g., Employment and Social Development Canada) would be for the testator (will-maker) to let the fiduciary know in advance they should also be contacting and informing the credit bureaus (e.g., Equifax, TransUnion).

- Some funeral homes have pre-planning options and services for not only memorialization, but also insurance to protect against identity theft after death.

- Seek out local agencies and government authorities for additional information about fraud, identity theft, and privacy awareness and prevention.

- Not sharing the news of a death on the deceased's social media accounts could be just as risky as sharing too much information. It is much better to have a carefully worded announcement with minimal information versus nothing at all. In a vacuum, the risk is someone other than the fiduciary will create and write a post that shares way too much personally identifiable information about the deceased.

Rely on the Basics for E-mail

With the proliferation of cybercrime, providing too much personal information is not a good thing. Undoubtedly, pulling back on providing specifics won't sit well with the genealogy community, but the risks aren't worth it. A client's obituary that has been distributed globally with personally identifiable information is inviting identity theft. Not uncommon are the tales of thieves reading obituaries and targeting homes when everyone is at the funeral. Your loved ones will be grieving enough when the deceased is gone; encourage your client not to add to their loss.

Just as we've learned about digital assets, testators (will-makers) will have to take control of pre-planning if they want their wishes to be honored. The digital age is marshaling the need for tighter integration between estate planning and estate administration, and it is no longer as simple as letting the fiduciary figure out. The estate lawyer and their testator client must spend time assessing risks, educating the fiduciary, and leaving more detailed guidance and instructions beyond the will. And so goes the story for every element of the estate administration process; obituaries in the digital age need a rethink.

Loyalty Rewards Programs and Gift Cards Matter in Estate Planning

It might seem absurd to begin an estate planning conversation by asking a client about their favorite loyalty, travel reward, or frequent shopper program, but it might be the perfect introductory conversation to the digital assets aspect of the client's estate plan. If you add in other similar digital assets such as gift cards or certificates and unclaimed balances on utility cards or online accounts, there could be significant financial value that clients have accumulated in transit, online payment, money transfer accounts, or digital wallets. With the growing proliferation of loyalty and rewards programs and gift cards, your client may have amassed more than they realize and probably have wishes about these aspects of their digital estate.

A Starting Point in Discovery: Where Are All These Loyalty and Rewards Programs and Gift Cards Coming From?

Modern-day points programs are considered to have started in the 1980s, with many retailers adopting these programs in the 1990s. The basic premise is a reward offer to consumers in exchange for personal information. Program participants provide personal data that is of tremendous value to the vendor (provider) in terms of customer retention and brand loyalty. With the emergence of the internet, consumers gained access to integrated types of money transfer accounts, digital wallets, and online payment systems such as PayPal, WePay, Google Pay, and Apple Pay. Gift cards followed a similar pattern with the first ones emerging in the late 1990s. It doesn't stop there. A cadre of companies has emerged to help clients evaluate and manage their loyalty programs or cash in their gift cards.

Technological Solutions Compound the Problem

It wasn't long before loyalty programs went digital and extended their value to include other services such as payment methods, and cross-vendor collection and reward opportunities. Loyalty and reward programs, with online accounts or mobile apps to track value and engagement with a particular vendor, are a product of services increasingly going digital.

Gift cards started out as physical cards, typically with an account number of the associated store and PIN or access code imprinted on the back. The balance was tracked on a ledger managed by the associated vendor. Today's e-gift cards are digital cards. When someone sends a gift card to another person, the account information of that gift card is stored digitally—no paper is exchanged. Similar to other digital assets, there may no longer be a paper trail, but these accounts are accumulating financial value along with some degree of personal information.

How Do Loyalty and Rewards Programs and Gift Cards Affect Our Clients' Estates?

- Loyalty and rewards programs and gift cards can have some form of exchangeable value, financial or otherwise, and these can add up. In the digital age, these assets are likely online and may not be easily found by the fiduciary.

- A client could be participating in numerous programs and have accounts with varying degrees of financial value. The fiduciary will want to close all of these accounts, particularly the accounts that maximize the value of the estate. Doing so not only meets the wishes of the testator (will-maker), but also protects privacy, and prevents cybercrime or identity theft of the estate. When enrolling in loyalty programs and signing up for online accounts, clients provide a wealth of personal information such as address, birthdate, phone number, e-mail, and other bits of personal information, the extent of which depends on the vendor.

- The vendor's terms of service stipulate what happens upon the account owner's death for loyalty programs as they do for most online accounts. Expect to be surprised. Most vendors reserve the right to change terms and conditions, so don't be alarmed if this happens.

- Closing all the deceased's online and offline accounts will be time consuming for the fiduciary. It's not yet a widespread norm for estate planners to consider these new types of assets, but fiduciaries will find there is no easy way to transfer balances or close accounts without contacting the provider and offering proof of the fiduciary's identity that satisfies the provider.

Reframing the Question: What Are the Key Recommendations About Loyalty and Rewards Programs and Gift Cards for Estate Planning Discovery?

- Encourage clients to create a digital assets inventory as part of their estate inventory and include their loyalty, rewards, and frequent shopper programs.

- Ferret out the big-ticket items. It wouldn't be improbable to assume that a client has at least one program in which they are saving up loyalty points or rewards. Just as with key physical assets, you'll want the client to highlight loyalty and reward programs they participate in with financial or exchangeable value. This step should include a review of the terms of service for high-value programs, cautioning clients that the terms could change.

- Pay particular attention to business owners, sole proprietors, or gig workers. Whose name are these loyalty programs in? What are the expectations or terms for award redemption? Are the terms for award redemption covered by business–employee agreements or business succession plans?

- Encourage the client to talk with their fiduciary and, if applicable, capture instructions in an appropriate legally recognized instrument. Without the client's guidance and direction, regardless of the volume of digital assets, estate administration can be complicated for fiduciaries. The fiduciary may be faced with how to divide a digital estate. Are the loyalty points to be split a number of ways, which might not be possible, or are they to go to one person? And if so, is there a value to be placed on their resulting estate allocation, or is it up to the fiduciary to decide? If anything, these decisions could also reduce the risk of beneficiary disputes, which are not always isolated to high-value assets but are just as likely to occur over low-valued and sentimental items.

- One option for clients is to donate unused loyalty points and gift cards to charity. Unused gift cards, loyalty points, and rewards can go a long way in assisting charities. Some vendors allow participants to make this choice within the program itself. Some programs are available and accessible within the provider themselves. Clients will have to contact the charity to determine if donating loyalty points is an option and obtain tax advice on whether these gifts are eligible for official donation receipts for post-death income tax.

- Talk to clients about privacy, cybersecurity, and identity theft. The conversation with the client involves the client's use of the internet, usage hygiene, maintenance, and good information technology practices. Encourage clients to close accounts they no longer use. Using or transferring balances when they accumulate protects client estates by avoiding points losing value or expiring, which can occur if the account is inactive. Good usage habits also protect against cybercrime and identity theft.

In its guidance on the secure online shopping experience, the UK's National Cyber Security Centre advises consumers not to give away too much personal information by being selective about what information they provide. This advice applies not only when making an online purchase, but also when setting up online accounts, including those of loyalty and rewards programs. Consider how much personal information is provided for even one hotel loyalty program.

- Beyond the technology management aspects of digital assets, there are considerations for estate administration, such as jurisdictional laws, taxes, and valuation for probate that apply, depending on their size, type, nature, collective value, and holder's use. As the volume, nature, and collective value of these types of digital assets change, it's prudent to stay current as laws and rules evolve.

When you consider the value individuals are accumulating in loyalty programs combined with the financial and sentimental value of other digital assets, estate values can add up. Be aware of the lack of consistency in terms of service among providers and identify significant digital assets in client portfolios as they may have worth upon death.

Case in Point: Digital Privacy Is a Matter for the Living and the Dead

In October 2017, Maureen Henry obtained a court order to gain access to her late son's social media accounts.

This tragic story in the digital age illustrates the painful state of our relationship with technology upon death, the digital custodians (online service providers), and the law—and when talking about digital privacy after death, we're also talking about estate planning. Digital privacy, when coupled with confidentiality and security, creates a triad compounding the complexity of issues for loved ones and the fiduciary.

This story is that of a young man who died in 2014 and his grieving mother's attempts to determine what happened. In her pursuit, she requested access to her deceased son's social media accounts and e-mail in the hope of gaining insight on why he died. Although an Ontario Superior Court judge issued an order in 2017 to give her access, two years later the media reported that two of the big tech giants based in the US had yet to comply, citing they will respond only to a US court order.

Although this story focused on the important implication of the unfulfilled court order and Maureen Henry's relationship with her son's service providers, which is defined by the terms of service, there are five major points related to estate planning worth addressing:

1. **Loved ones and fiduciaries will go to court to gain access to our e-mail and online photos:** Consider the years and cost involved when looking at this story. Without

a will and pre-planning, this could be the new reality in the digital age.

2. **Our digital lives are intertwined with our physical lives— one can take down the other:** In the twenty-first century home office, instead of corresponding by mail, virtually everything is done online from paying bills to making purchases to interacting with financial institutions. In the fiduciary role, be they laypersons, such as the deceased's children, or corporate designates, fiduciaries have long relied on print documents. A fiduciary's challenge in the digital era goes well beyond access to social media: it involves unravelling the connections between the client's physical and digital lives to ensure their estate needs are met.

3. **Both our physical and digital lives might leave only a virtual trail:** Estate and succession law is based on jurisdiction and so are many of the studies on the number of people with a will and estate plan. Jurisdiction-specific stats paint a pretty dire picture indicating less than half of people have a will or estate plan, and even fewer with an up-to-date one. When someone dies intestate, a court-appointed fiduciary determines what happens to their assets upon death. If the fiduciary can't find or access the deceased's assets, there will be nothing to pass on to loved ones.

4. **Consumer awareness regarding digital privacy on death needs to change:** As the number of cases like Maureen Henry's grow, it is unlikely consumers will remain content that their digital assets can't be transferred upon their death. As consumers gain awareness of this issue, they will demand digital custodians provide favorable terms of service upon the account owner's death along with pre-planning tools so that beneficiaries can be identified.

5. **Conflict of law happens when it isn't clear which laws and rules take priority in a particular situation:** For example, this could occur if we live in one country and

own property in another. Conflict of laws is more likely to occur with digital assets when we are dealing with global service providers.

Apps and online accounts need to provide more options regarding digital privacy wishes upon the account owner's death. Just as we have seen various constructs for physical asset estate planning, we need a variety of methods to help manage digital assets upon death. The tragic story of Maureen Henry and her search for understanding her son's death illustrates the need for tech companies and consumers to be better prepared and informed.

Chapter Five
The Digital Estate Planning Tsunami

"Estate 2K" for Digital Assets

In the midst of a pandemic, the evolutionary technology issues we've faced in the past seem so last century, like minor bumps in the road. It's as if we've been moving in slow motion compared to the lightning speed of digitization and disruption facing the estate industry and every other industry today. When dealing with previous challenges such as the emergence of the internet, the technology adaptation required to prepare for the year 2000 with the roll-over from two to four digits (Y2K), computer viruses, and the explosive growth in the dot-com bubble years, the technical issues were novel and material. Businesses invested millions of dollars in meeting marketplace expectations, addressing client requirements, leveraging innovation, and mitigating risk to prepare for each challenge. And, when you think about it, isn't helping clients address their personal planning requirements while mitigating risk what estate planners do?

Although this is not a book about the pandemic, the COVID-19 pandemic has changed (and continues to change) everything, and estate advisors are caught in the middle of clients with increased digital dependency, a heightened societal consciousness of mortality, and the practical realities of incapacity planning, will making, and estate planning.

Estate advisors are already experiencing a disruption, their own version of Y2K, because prior to COVID-19, a client might not have had much of digital footprint, but they do now. Today, a client's life undoubtedly includes a digital estate, fundamentally changing the role of the fiduciary. Estate advisors will now need to have an understanding of their client's digital assets in order to provide informed estate planning advice.

So what exactly is the estate industry's version of "Estate 2K"?

As discussed, all of us own a new class of assets called *digital assets* that can have value in the thousands of dollars, if you consider loyalty points, travel rewards, cryptoassets, blogs, and web domains. And if not financial value, then sentimental value, such as our digital photos, social media content, videos, and posts. We also go online to access details regarding our underlying physical assets and property rights, such as financial accounts, creating another aspect of our digital estate that is likewise invisible to estate administration.

Compounding existing challenges is the growing and massive client digital footprint. The volume and complexity of online accounts stands as further proof that we might need tech to manage our tech. Watch for #estatetech trending on social media in days to come as the conversation amplifies. With the emergence and increasing value of digital vaults, business processes and technological innovation will be needed to address the growing complexity associated with our personal and professional digital footprints becoming intertwined.

Fundamentally, the pandemic has pushed the boundaries of legacy paper-based processes associated with will, incapacity, and estate planning, leading to virtual court proceedings, remote will-signing, electronic wills, and electronic and digital signatures. To the extent that remote signing rules and virtual court proceedings take us to the brink of disruption, the required transformation of business processes and knowledge management in the estate industry is as yet not contemplated.

Given how dynamically the industry is unfolding, I will offer my forecast on what we can expect to see in the future.

Clarifying the Role of the Fiduciary

The fiduciary's role, whether that of an executor or estate trustee dealing with an estate or trust, or of an actor in situations of incapacity, became unhinged in the digital age. The traditional role and responsibilities of the fiduciary remain entrenched in jurisdiction-specific laws, with the powers outlined in legal and other recognized instruments. But digital assets are challenging all forms of legislation, including but not limited to will and estate succession, privacy, computer use, tax, other property rights (e.g., intellectual property), and laws across jurisdictions.

Fiduciary access laws, those jurisdiction-specific rules that govern what a fiduciary is allowed to do with digital assets upon incapacity or death, are new and evolving. Today's fiduciary will likely need current legal information and perhaps legal advice to navigate the ever-evolving legal landscape as it relates to digital assets. In addition to considering the laws in the client's jurisdiction, estate advisors also need to consider where the client's providers and certainly where the tech giants are based. Given that many of the tech giants are US based, looking at RUFADAA—US fiduciary access laws, and attempting to draw any conclusions on their impact on estate planning, there is one clear conclusion: Clients, regardless of their country of residence, will need to research, pre-plan, document, test, and update their estate planning assumptions for individual digital assets as things change.

As this book is about the technical management aspects of dealing with digital assets, it will not attempt to outline or keep up with what will be a galactic shift in the legal landscape. Suffice to say, the fiduciary cannot just pick up where the will-maker left off without being exposed to multiple legal ramifications. We already know and have described how contract law as it applies to provider terms of service has had a dramatic impact on many clients' digital assets.

If you want a practical reason for digital assets planning, consider this: How would a fiduciary know what a deceased person's usernames were unless they were clearly documented in a digital assets inventory by digital account? Take the following scenario whereby the fiduciary calls the customer service number of the tech provider where their mom had been writing and storing her memoirs. This is what a call transcript might look like between the fiduciary and the customer service center:

> Fiduciary: "My mom recently died, and she wrote her book using your platform. Can you give me all of the manuscript files?"
>
> Customer Service: "Hi, Fiduciary, I'm sorry to hear about your mom. What was her name?"
>
> Fiduciary: "Mary Jane Smith."
>
> Customer Service: "I don't see the username *Mary Jane Smith*. What was your mom's username and e-mail for this account?"
>
> Fiduciary: "Hmm … Ok, ok, I think it was *MJ Happy Times*."
>
> Customer Service: "I don't see any account under that name. What was her e-mail?"
>
> Fiduciary: "Gee, she had several e-mail accounts, how about MJ at [e-mail provider] dot com?"
>
> Customer Service: "Okay, I see we have that account, but the account owner's profile is incomplete. The billing information doesn't seem correct. Nor can I see any administrator or pre-planning options selected or updated. Can you prove your mom set up this account?"
>
> Fiduciary: "Hmm, I have a probated will, but she didn't leave a list of her usernames, and unfortunately, she didn't create a digital assets inventory."
>
> Customer Service: "I'm afraid you are going to have to

get a court order." Or: "Our company doesn't have any procedures for dealing with this type of situation, I'll have to take your contact information and call you back."

Another consideration in digital assets planning is taxes. Digital assets may have financial value, which could trigger a tax liability. Your clients might generate advertising revenue from a YouTube channel, own valuable web domains, receive blog or click revenue, sell their photographs or other art online, or own cryptocurrencies—which have raised the awareness of the financial value of digital assets in recent days. If your client has virtual assets, to what extent have you informed them of the need to track, trace, and document these digital assets for the purpose of leaving a tax liability trail?

The entire estate industry will need to respond to these challenges when consumer patience and tolerance wanes. Bereaved beneficiaries and families will not accept paying specialized legal and other advisor fees to draft court orders in an attempt to twist service providers' arms into providing access to data, funding technical endeavors to unlock encrypted computers, or recreating the tax paper trail of a digital photo. Simply put, who would be happy to pay thousands of dollars in legal fees to get access to a deceased person's e-mail because the estate advisor didn't tell the account user (testator/will-maker) to select pre-planning options or leave accessible information about their estates? Here are several other examples that illustrate account owners current relationship with the law and service providers:

- As reported by the Canadian Broadcasting Corporation, a widow in British Columbia waited months for the funds in her late husband's PayPal account to be transferred. This is not an isolated story. Collectively, we as estate advisors have an obligation to make clients aware of the potential value digital assets have within their portfolios and estates.

- This area of the law with respect to handling digital assets is new, evolving, and based on jurisdiction. There is the story from New York in which a surviving spouse had to secure a court order to gain access to his deceased husband's Apple iCloud account to retrieve family photos. The court order was secured two years after the deceased husband's death.

Preparing for Death Like a Project

Dealing with our digital lives requires us to apply some methodology. In *Your Digital Undertaker,* I outlined a project management–based checklist, which was applied to each aspect of the estate planning process. Refer to Chapter 2 of *Your Digital Undertaker*, "Getting Your Affairs in Order – Building Your Death Project in the Digital Age," to view this project management checklist. Here is the application of a project management framework and checklist to your client's personal digital assets in estate planning:

Scope: Why are you doing this?

How big are your client's digital shoes? Most people are surprised at the extent of their digital lives when they start to prepare a digital assets inventory or to use a (digital or paper) password manager for the first time.

Can the fiduciary fill your client's digital shoes? The volume of your client's digital assets, along with some of the unique challenges of handling them, can become a time-consuming task for any fiduciary, tech savvy or not. Your client will want to encourage the fiduciary to seek technical, legal, tax, and any other professional advice to deal with digital assets. In the same manner, they may need estate advice for physical assets or property rights.

However, there are also some digital shoes that your client's fiduciary should not be stepping into, such as online banking or e-mail if the client has decided that they want privacy in death—or any other area where the client has laid out specific wishes and preferences. In fact, as digital possessions are new and evolving, the best plan is for the client to review their digital assets with their advisor and the fiduciary when they are reviewing their will and estate plan.

Options and Trade-offs: What are the pros and cons?

Estate planning for digital assets requires the same rigor you'd apply when dealing with your client's physical assets. To keep it simple, consider these five key steps:

1. Understand what digital assets your client has using planning techniques similar to the consideration you might give for money or physical assets in estate planning. (i.e., create an inventory).

2. Develop a tech management plan appropriate to your client's digital assets situation. Depending on the complexity or use of a client's digital assets, they may need a separate tech management plan for each significant digital asset in addition to an inventory. This could include using pre-planning options and tools as they become available for your client's individual digital assets. Secure digital access information (e.g., passwords) separately from the inventory. Digital access information should be left in a secure manner that considers security guidance from providers, avoids potential criminal liability, and addresses privacy concerns or other actions that may contravene any terms of their licensing agreements. It is recommended that the client test and retest that the application of the documented digital access information and instruments work. Technology management is not a set-it-and-forget-it task, and any tech management plans created in support of estate planning will need to be maintained and revised as the technology or individual factors change.

3. Consider your client's digital wishes in the context of the constraints imposed by the providers (i.e., licensing agreements, legal property vs. what you don't own or have rights to, passwords and digital access).

4. Work with the appropriate legal advisor to determine options to address your client's digital wishes. Consider any differences in your client's wishes for incapacity versus death.

Document those choices and plans. Refer your client to a tax advisor if their digital assets have a financial value or tax attribute. Refer the client to qualified technical advice for significant or complicated digital assets.

5.   Review and determine how to give your client's fiduciary and attorney permissions and powers to deal with your digital assets (i.e., ask a legal advisor about a digital assets clause, an insert that addresses digital assets specifically, the powers and indemnities given to the fiduciary dealing with their administration and distribution, software account pre-planning options, if available, and other options recommended by your legal advisor for your jurisdiction). This is important as well, as there are likely many digital assets you have that might not be considered something you own from a legal perspective, as you may only have a non-transferrable license to use the account or digital asset and the service provider may terminate access upon receipt of a death notification or upon a stated period of inactivity. The basic role of a fiduciary is for the management of property that your client owns or have rights to. If your client's expect your fiduciary or attorney to deal with all your digital assets regardless of definition, you'll want to review that you have given them permission within the context of applicable jurisdictional law(s). For this advice, you will want to consult a legal advisor on how to address your specific situation and your specific types of digital assets. By the way, this is not just a problem for digital assets. Physical assets have this issue as well in terms of what is considered property, and who owns specific property (e.g., pets, genetic or reproductive material).

Preferences and Costs: What do you need and what's it going to cost?

Making a list may be inconvenient, but at least it isn't expensive. Remember, computers fail, hardware crashes, and technology becomes obsolete. Anyone who has had to recover data from a dead computer or a soggy smartphone either cursed themselves for not having a backup of their data or gave themselves a pat on the back because they backed up their data. What's your client's backup plan for the fiduciary to get your client's estate information? Even if your client was super organized and left incredible digital instructions, because technology is technology and can fail or expire, your client will want to consider the backup plan for their digital assets.

Procurement of Professional Services: The future is here.

The digital age will impact your client's estate planning, from considering client wishes for their digital assets to recommending that a client engage legal advice and preparing the fiduciary to potentially engage specialized technical services. Clauses can be added to legal documents to address your client's digital assets. A digital assets inventory, or just a simple list of what your client has, is good information when making or updating your client's will and power of attorney (POA).

Risks: What are the risks? What are the backup plans?

How a client manages their digital assets when they are alive will have a profound impact on privacy and data security after they are gone. You'll want to encourage your client to pay attention to their digital assets in life, securing and protecting them.

Communication: It is on a need-to-know basis and someone needs to know!

For all that is good and convenient about the digital age, it poses real challenges for your client's estate planning and eventually for the fiduciary. I've spent a lot of time in this chapter on considerations for pre-planning and what the fiduciary might face in dealing with your client's digital assets. The same challenges apply to other fiduciary roles, such as trustees or those who are the attorney (for your client's power of attorney), should your client become incapacitated. If your client is no longer able to remember their password, it will present significant challenges for others who have to step in to manage their digital affairs. Perhaps when your client reviews their digital assets inventory and wishes with the fiduciary, consider including your client's attorney in the conversation.

Implications for Estate Planning and Estate Administration

Traditional estate planning, as a set of business processes, is often segmented from estate administration. In the estate industry, there is no such term as *estate management* that encapsulates these two worlds. Perhaps the simple reason for this is that generally in the past, an average estate wasn't that complicated. The fiduciary would likely have found the advance care plan or incapacity directives, the will, and/or estate plans. They would have gathered up papers from a home office and begun their administration duties. If no such paperwork existed, court orders, based on jurisdictionally legislated succession laws, would direct the distribution of the estate.

As illustrated in *Your Digital Undertaker*, the twenty-first century home is now managed online with e-mail, and the internet is the foundation of our new home office. In the confines of these traditionally disconnected categories—estate planning and estate administration—how does one have the digital implication conversation?

When I am invited to present at client events and webinars, I begin the digital assets exploration from the end. From the lens of the fiduciary, acting as a project manager, they must manage a project they may not understand, engage with advisors they've never worked with, and play digital detective in deciphering the deceased's life, all the while grieving the loss of a loved one.

Comparing a 1980s home office to today's home office, I paint a picture with several estate administration scenarios to illustrate the estate planning implications. The conversation isn't just about a new asset class called digital assets, it is also about what the internet broke, as covered in Chapter One, and the evolving role of the fiduciary in the digital age.

Estate Administration

Consider the case of a corporate fiduciary who works for a trust company: The client dies, and the extended-care facility where they last lived hands over a cardboard box of the deceased's digital devices. Inside the box is a mobile phone, laptop, and a digital assets inventory listing their favorite apps and accounts.

Here are the process considerations.

- In the absence of charging cables that work with the client devices, how will you plug in these devices?
- How will you approach deactivating their online accounts, stop the payment of any online subscription services, and handle the digital assets (such as photos) according to the testator's wishes?
- In all likelihood, the IT policy at work states that you are prohibited from connecting foreign devices to your internal network, for the sake of cybersecurity. You should also consider whether or not you want devices from an unknown origin connecting to your home network.
- Considering this use case, a firm must establish policies, practices and likely tools for accessing data in these digital devices or accessing cloud-based digital assets via these devices during estate administration.

Our Intertwined Physical and Digital Lives

Suppose your client is an author, musician, composer, photographer, or other creator. You may be familiar with intellectual property rights associated with copyright, trademarks, and royalties, having considered those elements during client estate planning. But there is a further planning conundrum when physical property rights intertwine with the digital world. Consider the risks to your estate planning discovery process when tech is part of the equation.

- Did you ask the client where they keep the information supporting their copyrighted work, copies of draft works, and completed manuscripts?

- What about the filing of copyright or trademarks? What if your client's registration certificates are received electronically or trapped in e-mail and not printed out?
- What if in the digital age your client now saves all this information, their work-in-progress, and final work product in an e-mail account, a cloud account, or encrypted drive?
- What if your client isn't using online tools or platforms the way they were intended? What if your loved one was writing a book and saving their manuscript drafts in e-mail instead of another digital format?
- There are additional technical management steps and documentation required to adequately protect these types of digital assets and property rights.
- Questions such as, Will the storage source for the manuscript, music, digital art, photographs, and copyrights be accessible to the fiduciary in order for them to fulfill the directives in the will or estate plan? Are there unencrypted backup copies stored safely, such as in a safety deposit box or with a third-party custodian?

A client's intentions could be completely frustrated because you, as the estate advisor, didn't take the estate planning conversation one step further into the client's use of technology in managing those traditional property rights.

The Pandemic Digital Experiment

Your client is an active older adult over the age of 65 who is familiar with technology such as e-mail and other applications, having used them at work. When they retired, they became engaged more with their community, visiting family and friends, or "snowbirding" in the winter. The pandemic hit, and they, being part of an identified vulnerable population, remained indoors. At first, they found amusement in getting some of their long-ignored tasks complete. As the pandemic wore on, they took up a hobby or expanded an existing one. It wasn't long before their hobby grew into several social media groups and an idea to sell their hobby output online.

Before the summer hit, they had a platform to sell their hobby projects, a payment provider, and a social media account to promote their products.

- The client now has not only expanded their digital footprint, but also ventured beyond the personal realm into the business realm, online marketplace or the platform economy.
- Have you as an estate advisor considered asking the client how many hours they devote to their pursuits, how many products they plan to sell, and how much they earn? Because during estate administration, the fiduciary is going to need to know.
- Is there a balance of funds sitting in the online payment provider platform?
- Are there likely to be liabilities or outstanding orders on the client's website or chosen platform?
- How will the fiduciary access the deceased person's artwork, the draft manuscripts, or the half-composed song if they do not have authorized access into these cloud accounts?

Tech Pre-planning Options

Very few service providers offer pre-planning options for account owners' personal accounts; however, I've discussed that Google and Facebook were the first two tech giants to offer pre-planning options for personal accounts. I make the distinction between pre-planning options for personal accounts and those potentially available to businesses. In 2019, a Comparitech survey indicated that two-thirds of Facebook users hadn't used the Legacy Contact feature.

These examples should illustrate the importance of clients expressing their wishes about their digital afterlife to their fiduciary. I haven't given an exhaustive list of examples, because the minute this book is published, options from the service providers will no doubt change. A further reason we need to care about what is happening is to establish the de facto standard. Just as with every other industry, what happens first likely sets the tone of what happens in the future.

A reminder why advisors should care about social media in estate planning is that, first, clients will have wishes about what happens to their digital content; second, a client's digital assets are a panoply of information for cybercrooks upon the client's death; and third, according to the new Digital 2020 October Global Statshot Report, more than 50% of people in the world use social media—a staggering four out of eight billion. And given that over 70% of North Americans use Facebook, social media is an easy place to start the conversation.

James Norris of the Digital Legacy Association reminds us to back up or download information regularly if the content held on these platforms is important. From these examples, it's evident there is not much choice other than closing an account after death, and when that happens, the data is gone. Think about the value which will be lost in all those blog posts and social media accounts.

The pre-planning options available for personal accounts are more restrictive than you would think in terms of estate planning options. Without consumer consultation, and collaboration between regulatory bodies and industry, we will continue to see different and limited options, with a divergence of definitions and choices. However, what we understand for physical property and physical property rights similarly applies to digital assets: it all depends on the client's circumstances, the way they have chosen to use the items, and their preferences upon incapacity and/or death.

Relatively speaking, the process for deactivating online accounts, including social media, is simple, and the fiduciary won't need passwords to do so, but there might be a lot of accounts which would be time consuming for the fiduciary—depending, of course, on the information accessible to the fiduciary on the digital accounts the deceased has, and that the deceased's profile is accurate and up to date. However, it is a completely different ball game if your fiduciary wants to access the data or transfer the assets as per your client's wishes, such as wanting the data to remain accessible or memorialized.

It is my sincere wish that after reading this book, readers will be familiar with the comprehensive definition of a digital asset, which is that a digital asset has many of the same complex characteristics as physical assets and property, such as financial and sentimental value.

Your clients may have intentions for not only their physical assets, but also their growing inventory of digital assets, which could include family photos, web domains, or loyalty points.

A Further Comment About the Work Ahead for Service Providers

Marketplace awareness is low, and consumers will need to make their requirements known in order for things to change. But when they do, conversely, consumers will need to be made aware that you don't flip a switch to "turn on" pre-planning features. Service providers have work to do to define policies and then potentially provide options for account owners.

For service providers: Having led project teams at IBM, I know large enterprise systems are difficult to architect, build, implement, and maintain. Furthermore, I know global enterprise IT projects that cross boundaries are complex and many fail before they even start. Competing jurisdictional rules, time zones, multi-stakeholder agreements, consensus or decision-making requirements make the process exhausting—even the best teams have been crushed under the pressure. It takes a unique consulting perspective to navigate, facilitate, and lead these kinds of efforts.

I know from my time in government serving in the Royal Canadian Air Force that every policy, regardless of its purpose (for business management or client relationship management), often requires inordinate energy and effort to develop and maintain its currency over its life cycle.

Software development has a similar life cycle: from requirements gathering to architectural design to development and testing. One thing that wasn't obvious at first but became more obvious throughout my career was the downstream cost to maintain or change policies and code.

Simply put, if you spend a dollar, a pound, or a euro on just one line of code or policy statement, you'll spend hundreds or even thousands more on it over the life cycle of that code. The downstream cost of people, resources, and support structures is often forgotten or not understood when maintaining a single line of code or policy statement.

In practical terms, service providers need administrators, training manuals, and exception processes to deal with challenges in servicing those policy statements, creating a challenge for all service providers, particularly when those services are free to the end user.

Tech Management Awareness

Advisors, organizations, and professional practices, processes, and tools will need to be updated to address your clients' growing digital inventories. Here are five tips to consider when planning a client's digital assets (the first four are from the *STEP Journal* article "The Digital Tsunami").

1. Learn about the client's digital life

"Ask your client if they use e-mail or social media, and how they share family photos. Look for digital assets of both financial and sentimental value. Encourage them to identify their top three digital assets that would have the greatest impact if they were lost or inaccessible."

As a reminder why advisors should care about social media during estate planning, clients will have wishes about their content, such as photos on these sites where there is a wealth of information for cybercrooks to mine from the accounts of deceased individuals.

2. Differentiate between digital assets

"Explore how the client uses those three key digital assets and research their associated licensing agreements or terms of service (if they exist), as well as any pre-planning options that the service provider offers. If pre-planning is not offered, ask what paperwork the fiduciary will have to provide."

- Have the client make a list of the important assets in their life including digital assets, or better yet, used the STEP Inventory referenced in Chapter Two.
- Working with the client's top three digital assets, investigate the terms of service agreement associated with those accounts and any pre-planning options from the service providers.
- Have the client review their list with their fiduciary.
- If the client has digital assets of significance (such as websites), a qualified technology advisor can help identify the components and assist the client in determining options and creating a tech management plan in addition to other applicable estate planning components.

3. Seek appropriate advice

"A legal advisor can advise a client on how to capture wishes and preferences about those digital assets (e.g., jurisdictional laws, fiduciary access, and will inserts or clauses). For complex digital estates, advisors are wise to seek expertise in areas such as technical, tax, and cross-border requirements as appropriate. Remember, even if the tech experts are on the fiduciary's side, due to jurisdiction-specific fiduciary access laws, they might not be legally authorized to access digital assets, even if they hold the passwords."

- During estate instrument drafting, ensure estate planning covers the client's digital and non-digital life, giving the fiduciary powers to deal with both.
- As part of the estate planning process, review the inventory for both physical and digital assets, listing what they own and what is important. Have them reach out to their financial

planner, retirement planner, insurance broker, technical advisor, financial institution, gift planner, or legal advisor as appropriate during the process.

- Have you addressed significant digital assets identified by the client with the same rigor as significant physical assets and property rights?
- Existing wills need periodic updating, which is a good time to ensure that digital properties are listed with appropriate management instructions. Inserting a digital assets clause is a good first step when revising a will, but such a clause is insufficient on its own for estate planning.

Digital assets, similar to physical assets and property rights, need to be addressed separately for both will/estate plans and advance care (living) situations. A client may have different preferences, depending on the type of digital asset, and a qualified legal advisor can help address how to legally document wishes, preferences, and powers for the fiduciary to deal with digital assets in the case of incapacity and/or death. There may be additional estate planning requirements depending on the type, significance, and use of a particular digital asset, thus the need to understand the service provider terms of service requirements.

4. Discuss tech management strategies with the client

"Encourage the client to consider user or technology management steps. These include documenting, testing or transferring digital assets before incapacity or death, and identifying and mitigating other risks that might prevent the fiduciary from carrying out their wishes."

- Suggest to the client they may want to document, test, or transfer digital assets before incapacity or death, and discuss any other risks that might inhibit the fiduciary from carrying out the decedent's wishes.
- Leverage the project management steps outlined in Chapter Two to address risks and issues associated with a specific technology or digital asset.

- Technology and digital assets introduce a new expertise required to support the advisor and client in their estate planning process. Have you built relationships with the technology industry and service providers? Do you know where to refer a client if they need specialized technical expertise unique to their circumstances for handling their wishes and digital asset(s)?

- Technology and digital assets evolve rapidly and are often tied to infrastructure or platforms that are constantly being updated. Updates and revisions to the technical management planning aspects of digital assets in estate planning will need more frequent updates than traditional estate planning constructs.

- Case in point: A web domain is the name of a website. A Uniform Resource Locator (URL) is a specific address where someone can find a website online. A website is what people interact with when they get there. In other words, when you buy a (web) domain, you have registered the name of your site; you'll need to acquire web hosting services for your site to appear publicly and then you'll need to add content on that website. All in all, before you know it, you'll have several digital accounts, to manage the (web) domain, to provide navigation directions, to maintain the content of the website, to manage any associated social media, and potentially to manage other applications that interact with the website or point to other resources.

5. Have the client prepare their fiduciary.

Preparing the fiduciary is sound advice offered by estate advisors. What that means and to what degree obviously depends on an individual's circumstances. Advisors find themselves constantly reminding clients to prepare a will, create an inventory, update beneficiary designations, and talk to their fiduciary. Professionals, including advisors will need to rethink how they contract, engage, and communicate this important topic with clients in the digital age.

The reality in transitioning from paper to digital requires leaving a trail and preparing the client to protect the value of their estate.

- The digital age and our use of the internet means there is no longer a paper trail. This fact alone will frustrate a testator's intentions. Further, digital assets by their nature are virtual or stored on hard drives and unlikely to be found without pre-planning and communication in advance with the fiduciary. Add jurisdiction-specific laws and providers' terms of service, and the situation will hinder access or transfer of digital assets after death.

- I share this with client audiences by saying, "Okay, let me get this right, your life is not complicated. But you are going to leave a perhaps inexperienced person, who has unlikely dealt with lawyers, taxes, or government agencies, to figure out your life, manage the project of closing down your life, without anyone to talk to on this project. How's that going to work out? When have you ever taken on a project and not been allowed to ask any questions or get help from the person who asked you to do the project?"

- It may seem trivial, but one of the best and simplest things a testator can do is prepare their families by leaving memories for loved ones. Photos that used to be kept in physical albums are now stored on phones or on the cloud. Will they be accessible after death?

Case in Point: The Need for Pre-planning Best Practices

The sudden death in 2018 of the CEO of one of Canada's largest cryptocurrency exchanges made global news when he died without allegedly leaving anyone the digital keys to the company's cryptocurrency wallet. It is estimated that some CAD$180 million of clients' cryptocurrency reserves were lost. Certainly, the news garnered lots of interest, given it was about cryptocurrencies and involved large sums of money. But this story also serves as a timely reminder to any advisor involved in estate planning regarding the proper management of digital assets.

That is a story of the need for pre-planning best practice. Without a recovery password or adequate pre-planning, even the best tech professionals and court orders may never get into the CEO's encrypted laptop—if, indeed, the keys are stored on it at all. Then, to add insult to injury, as cryptocurrencies are both unregulated and managed by experts in a decentralized way, there is no central help desk that to reset the password, nor can the company's stakeholders turn to the law for help. Beyond the sensational elements of this story, it is a stark reminder of the implications of all the mundane digital assets we own such as e-mail, social media, and our intertwined business and personal lives.

Looking for more information about this case from an estate planning perspective and the technical management elements? I'd recommend reading the Quadriga CX four-part series published by *The Lawyer's Daily* (August–September 2020) and the *STEP Journal* article "The Digital Tsunami Meets Estate Administration." The area of estate planning for cryptoassets will certainly unfold.

For a lay person's description of how cryptocurrencies work, I'd recommend reading the gift card analogy in the Appendix to Chapter 7 of *Your Digital Undertaker*.

For a starting point in cryptoassets in estate planning, I'd recommend reading Pamela Morgan's *Cryptoasset Inheritance Planning*.

There is a very real and practical element to the technological management of digital assets. Without the necessary pre-planning, all the cybersecurity measures put in place during a client's lifetime will act as barriers imposed on the fiduciary. Estate advisors might be best advised to approach pre-planning of significant digital assets by assuming that passwords will not be available or usable for whatever reason: legal, technical, or otherwise.

Chapter Six
An Eye to the Digital Future

Five Things About the Future of Estate Planning

Understanding digital assets on their own as a new class of assets is a convenient and simple way to begin the awareness journey. But the reality is that the internet broke estate planning and estate administration when paper-based processes such as will creation became automated. Bottom line: everything online is a digital asset.

Thus, where to start?

One must realize that everything in the estate industry is a candidate for digitization, and the pandemic accelerated this change. To the extent that every organization had to develop their own Y2K plan or dot-com bubble plan to navigate the technical challenges of the past, so too will the industry need to develop a digitization plan to address the monumental changes that are about to unfold in the death care and estate industries.

Certainly, one could start small, just by addressing digital assets as a new class of existing client assets. Deal with digital assets as electronic records: e-mail, social media, or cryptoassets. Develop a framework for updating business processes, policy, tools, and practices, and a maintenance process to deal with the ever-growing digital inventories.

Have a strategic eye to the future. Begin the organizational conversation developing programs and initiatives aimed at digitization. Find the sweets spots of success that leapfrog the competition, while staying current with what will become the new normal for business operations to retain competitive necessity.

These are the areas I see changing:

Estate planning: We enjoy technology in our lives, but digital assets become difficult to access after death for all the reasons I've outlined in this book.

Because our physical assets and physical property rights have become intertwined with our digital lives, and our underlying assets are accessed digitally, they too have become constrained by the current estate planning paradigm.

Central to the estate and incapacity planning process is an inventory of a client's assets—digital and non-digital (physical). That inventory is then wrapped with what are essentially paper-based business processes and separate, often disconnected estate planning components (tax, legal, philanthropy, insurance, finance, technical) to produce an estate plan. How complete that estate plan, and its associated transaction, is entirely dependent on the integrated planning capability of one or more estate planners, the tools they use, and the degree to which the client actively participates in the process.

If any client ever truly achieves such an ideal plan, the estate plan and its bits and pieces are typically dated the day it is published. The new estate planning paradigm will force the entire financial and estate industry to evolve such that an estate plan becomes a living, breathing encapsulation of one's life and legacy, and is capable of evolving as the client ages.

The estate plan will be iterative, will evolve or be added to as life unfolds, and will be able to withstand new planning paradigms, changing estate offering components, and new or changing advisors. How it will be instantiated will likely be driven by the platform and offerings, and success will be measured by beneficiaries who provide feedback through the incapacity and estate administration processes.

Estate administration: Corporate trust companies and

professional fiduciaries will be challenged to innovate or be sur-passed by emergent service providers who offer more integrated digital services and offerings.

We've begun to see tech entrepreneurs emerge in the asset inventory and digital vault arena with digital estate vaults, which are loosely akin to password managers, incorporating estate planning requirements that meet jurisdiction-specific legal and other requirements.

It is, therefore, only a figurative leap to further tech innovation and business process evolution that addresses the data integra-tion and end-to-end delivery model that the future consumer mar-ketplace will demand. When this happens, I believe this market shift will obliterate the traditional trust company model.

Future estate administration will be measured by the degree to which an estate plan can be executed and addressed in a timely manner. Do not expect beneficiaries to remain silent during this evolution. In this future state, family members and friends who are appointed as fiduciaries will not likely undertake the role without hiring a services integration partner.

As such, clients, regardless of their age or stage in life, can expect that services involving aspects of financial or estate plan-ning will offer tools, services, or advice on how their holdings or information will integrate through to estate administration. Client expectations will change, and they will expect and demand tools and services that capture and integrate their inventories through-out their lives.

The cost of these future estate administration services providers will scale exponentially to the degree to which planning was done upfront, and then will normalize as assets and detection services emerge to compete in this space.

Prior to the pandemic, I said, "The future executor is a digital executor." Fast forward, and I can safely say, "Today's executor is a digital executor," and "Today's fiduciary is a digital fiduciary." Perhaps more importantly for this audience, "Today's advisor must also be a digital advisor."

End-to-end data and solution integration in the estate industry: Expect clients to seek integration between estate and incapacity planning and estate and incapacity administration business processes. Individuals will no longer accept the past norm of creating a will, tossing it over the proverbial wall and leaving it to the fiduciary to figure out.

Without a paper trail documenting one's assets, the likelihood of loss increases dramatically for not only digital assets, but also physical assets bound up in digital trails. We will need new business processes and tech to manage our tech for our growing digital footprint.

Consumers will challenge the basic tenets of will and estate planning where they will break away from the traditional approach of static documentation to the expectation of real-time update capabilities capturing life transitions and events.

Expect the paper-based estate planning process to break when new solutions emerge providing seamless traceability from asset acquisition, use, and disposal, to transfer after incapacity and/ or death.

The death positive movement's goal is to raise our death literacy rate as people engage in meaningful conversations with their loved ones. By doing so, they gain clarity on their end-of-life wishes as they begin the process of planning. The calamity and helplessness felt by caregivers dealing with loved ones during the pandemic alone will fuel a revolution.

As a result of our new global paradigm, death literacy will grow, and clients will become more comfortable with the conversation about end of life as they do about retirement. Clients will want to make plans earlier in life and document with greater clarity their advance care directives. The global personal experience with the pandemic will raise valid and important questions as clients question and attempt to gain assurance that their advance care and end-of-life wishes will be met.

Transformation and digitization of the estate industry: Accelerated by the pandemic, organizations, societies, the charitable and non-profit sector, financial, consulting, and other institutions that make up the death care and estate industries will race to create new business models mapping out the unfolding frontier of digitization, and then build or procure solutions and platforms to meet these business and client estate requirements.

Tech entrepreneurs, who have been nibbling at the edges of automating basic estate business processes and functions, will bust open the seams of tech incubators. The revolution will start with front- and back-office process transformation inside estate management organizations, then extend to the judiciary processes, followed by consumer expectations for the same ease of use and accessibility consumers experience on other industry and sector platforms. The estate industry's digital transformation has already begun as organizations, companies, and advisors have been adopting point-specific estate business tools and solutions (e.g., online inventory apps and solutions). Expect tech entrepreneurs and service providers to pick up steam as electronic wills are jurisdictionally legislated, and the market awakens.

The estate industry will revolutionize when the evolution extends to integrated estate platforms which will emerge and integrate estate business processes, firm practices, client requirements and extend the digital data hand-off from the will-maker (testator) to their fiduciary and advisors on both sides of the incapacity and death fences. Clients and the marketplace will expect these platforms to be accessible and evolve throughout their lives, address all their assets including digital and integrate into their estate planning requirements of financial, insurance, funeral, memorialization, gifting, technical and every aspect of their lives that require planning and transition to their beneficiaries. Companies and firms will race to partner or create platforms, to not only deal with the essentials, but offer cost efficiency, ease of use and capture ever-evolving client wishes and preferences.

Client home office information technology transformation. In the industrial or organizational context, we often talk about the information highway or the need to consider and treat technology as an essential resource. We are long past technology as mere table stakes.

As our personal lives continue to be digitized and integrated with technology, we will see the need to engage tech support to not only help us select technology and fix our point-specific tech issues, but also address our ongoing maintenance needs. Yet we haven't contemplated the complex challenge of creating a support system for successfully transitioning our estate plans in a tech-heavy home environment. In companies with an IT department, we'd look to support from the IT department to handle our technology needs (new, old, and uncontemplated). In the work environment, there is continuity in IT delivery, ensuring uninterrupted operations supported by practices and policies as employees and clients come on board or depart.

So what do we do at home for our own IT department? It appears we predominately do it ourselves or we rely on friends and family for help when needed, or we buy point-specific services when things go wrong. We might have dealt with the sales face of a provider to purchase an item, be that hardware, software, or services.

In reality, we haven't contemplated the business succession of our own home tech. We may not have realized the number of digital accounts we have, nor how integrated our home tech is, pushing it to an IT system. A website or a blog alone has a number of dimensions from hosting and security to content management. Or, we might have considered our only IT being e-mail or social media, but now our homes are interconnected as an *internet of things* where opening our cars or adjusting our home thermostats requires a smartphone. As such, our lives just got more tech dependent.

Given the ferocious pace with which we are adopting and using technology, in many regards we'll also need an eye to cost, maintainability, and transferability, I believe that in the future we will see home IT as a service offering, along the lines of what is available for businesses, which is an end-to-end, integrated, and continuous IT support system including desk-side help. If you look to high-net-worth clients or multigenerational families who procure family office offerings that include services to manage their day-to-day lives, perhaps there is a new integrated digital home office offering that extends to IT and is available to a broader spectrum of clients.

As I have argued, I have been increasingly concerned about the myths and prevailing advice on managing or planning for our digital lives when some of this so-called guidance suggests the answer is as simple as sharing passwords with friends and family. I've even seen advice recommending an uninformed idea of a password swap as a simple fix to the digital assets in estate planning problem. These superficial suggestions couldn't be less valid when you consider basic technical best practices, never mind jurisdictional law or service provider terms of service. However, this cast-off advice might be explainable considering how we manage our home IT today.

If clients rely on their friends and family to manage their home IT while they are alive, why not let them deal with their digital lives upon the client's death? This advice is often wrapped around invented terms to legitimize the family member appointed as a digital steward, digital guardian, or digital executor without regard for how to do this from an estate planning perspective with compliant legal instruments and service provider contracts as discussed in Chapters 2 and 4. We will need other recognized, practical, and legal ways to deal with our digital assets beyond uninformed notions where digital assets are treated as one size fits all.

What individuals and the estate industry will soon realize is that our home IT and our personal digital lives need the same end-to-end integrated support common in many professional work environments. Some may consider this thinking as overkill, but I posit home IT management is required to ensure personal continuity, as applied to the individual person in the same vein as we consider business continuity in an organizational context, particularly if we have wishes about the effective transfer or closure of our digital environments.

Picture a continuum: think of IT management services examples such as Best Buy's Geek Squad Services or Nerds on Site® (Technology Partners); virtual assistants; or the support from the tech behemoths—now extend this support to that offered by a future-state service provider that virtually manages home IT systems, readying them for transfer or closure upon the account owner's death.

The use of technology at home is no longer an option. Technology is essential in our daily lives and we are dependent on its applications. Our home equipment and our personal processes to select and maintain technology will need to improve substantially if consumers are to not only protect, but also leverage the platforms and innovation they will expect in the estate industry.

Estate advisors will not only need to be tech savvy, but also educators providing offerings that foster a more robust home technology ecosystem with a more secure client–advisor engagement model. As an example during lockdown, if you encouraged a client to use online banking or perform other financial transactions electronically, did you ask about the quality of their equipment, the need for following IT best practices, or the need to keep their technology current? Did you offer or refer the client to a reputable service provider or technical advisor?

With clients living longer lives, the focus on incapacity planning and the quality and security of one's life may drive a more balanced estate planning conversation between advance care plans and traditional estate plan.

The pandemic has forced everyone to deal with technology. The generation that is well into retirement may have thought they could avoid using e-mail altogether, but they have found themselves videoconferencing with loved ones and health care providers.

Digital literacy will be at least equitable to the need for financial literacy, for today's testator (will-maker). Prior to the pandemic, I said, "Technology is the new player at the estate planning table." Fast forward to now, and I say, "Technology must be an integrated partner in the estate planning conversation".

Case in Point: The Digital Transformation Path Starts With One Change

We are on the precipice of the largest disruption to date of any industry.

What will be the tipping point?

The estate industry is undergoing a digital transformation not just because our clients own digital assets, nor because of the emotional and financial value placed on those assets. It's too simple to blame the internet for the industry's digital transformation, even though the web has obliterated the paper trail in our client's home office, disrupting estate administration processes and the role of the fiduciary.

The digital transformation could be because there is a great deal of money at stake fueling the next generation of integrated estate banking. Or because our clients will expect the same level of digitization they now get from other sectors that have figured out secure client engagement tasks such as digital and electronic signatures. Further, they will expect the current disparate process of will and estate planning to be integrated with estate administration in a manner that facilitates the role for the fiduciary and optimizes the value of the entire estate.

More likely, the COVID-19 pandemic will play its part in driving us to recognize our own morbidity and the need for end-of-life and estate planning conversations.

We will want to point to a single event to explain the big bang crystalizing the estate industry's transformation. When I'm asked what that event will be, I point to the backbone of estate planning—the will. The notion that legislation will support an electronic will changes everything. Because once a will is digitized, the data and process ecosystem surrounding that basic building block from client interaction right through to the back office of the courts provides the groundwork for transformation.

The pandemic has accelerated change, as a crisis often does. We were forced to examine how things were done and remote will-signing and remote court proceedings define evolution in this industry.

You might think an electronic will is something coming to another jurisdiction near you, as in, "I don't need to worry about it for a long time," but we've passed the digital threshold of client expectations. This will be a client demand. For example, if some jurisdictions have electronic wills and others have paper-based wills, what would be the most efficient process for the resolution of cross-jurisdiction property issues when different jurisdictions have different processes?

We're headed toward a new era of electronic wills, and subsequently everything else will be digitized, including drafting and handling of the will, management of assets, transference of assets and communication with the fiduciary/advisors. In the future, both physical and digital assets will be digitally connected to an estate, will, trust, or other estate planning construct, and perhaps even to one's birth. From my experience of having led major e-business projects for IBM, including projects that digitized business processes in financial, retail, and government processes (including one that digitized a land title process), if history is a predictor, everything is on the table for digitization.

So where to next? Every IT or digitization project starts with an examination of business processes, and the estate industry's transformation project will be no different. What's different than projects of old is that implementation will likely be outsourced and cloud-based, but the motivation should be the same. It's the right thing to do for the client.

Chapter Seven

The Electronic Will Changes Everything

The pandemic may have accelerated the digitization conversation, but when the electronic will is legislated jurisdictionally, it will change everything. Client expectations about applying technology to processes such as wills and estate plans requires jurisdictions to legislate new laws and incorporate new rules to address these marketplace demands. The pandemic has accelerated the digitization conversation in all aspects of the estate industry and within its associated business models and processes.

Jurisdiction-specific estate legislation and court processes have been leveraging technology, the internet, and digital innovation to deal with social distancing and other public health and government measures. More so dramatically, the entire life cycle of the estate industry is being challenged to evolve, adapt, and innovate with technology resulting in an accelerated digitization of the entire estate industry.

Digital assets may simply be electronic records, but they are the digital gateway to clients' lives and estates. Technology has innovated clients' workplaces and transformed their homes. Because they have digital devices and digital "things," they now have a digital estate or digital legacy to consider as part of will and estate planning.

The role of the fiduciary has changed and what people expect of the death care and estate industries will change. The death positive movement emerged in an effort to help individuals become death literate and understand their choices in end-of-life planning, along with social media providing new ways to express grief and celebrate the lives of loved ones.

We will be the first generation to transfer our digital lives and digital footprint to our loved ones, and we have all relied on the internet to assist us during the COVID-19 pandemic. Consider how many of us signed up for new accounts for grocery delivery, curbside pickup, physician services, and online socializing. Then there are those of us who started new hobbies or migrated our work and school lives online.

Case in Point: The Closing Argument

We enjoy technology, but digital assets become difficult to access after death. My objective in this book was to paint a picture of the evolving digital estate landscape to increase the reader's level of awareness and comfort of where digital assets fit in this important topic.

In the context of the industry's digital transformation, we can expect estate professionals and organizations to begin talking about the broader play where we'll see language, definitions, contextual framework diagrams, and terminology emerging to help us navigate the digital journey. Fundamentally, every aspect of the estate business is being challenged to automate, digitize and innovate. The pandemic increased our reliance on technology and the internet to navigate our worlds where now the idea of remote will-signing or electronic wills is part of mainstream conversation.

I'm sure you've already seen and may have used the term *digitization of the estate industry*, which is often used for any technical transformation that is expected to happen overnight. As we know from other industry experiences, overnight transformation is not the case. We are in for a five- to ten-plus-year journey as various aspects of an estate organization's processes, tools, and tech evolve in response to market demand and consumer expectations as various jurisdictions' laws mature. The life cycle speed to digitize the estate industry will likely be faster than other industries, but there is still a life cycle to any transformation. On one hand, as estate advisors, we will certainly welcome that clients will now embrace the need for will and estate planning and expressing their wishes for advance care and end of life. Further, this transformation opens a much wider cross-generational conversation because tech is still cool, no matter where you are on life's continuum.

On the other hand, this transformation will also pose a significant leadership challenge for advisors, their profession, and organizations as we help clients navigate the upheaval that any digital transformation will cause. In the end, if we face the challenge with optimization, take some risk to learn about and embrace the digital and test the conversation with clients, we might find the subject not only enhances our existing client relationships, but also opens the doors to new opportunities, partnerships, and other prospects.

In summary, this book is focused on digital assets specifically in the estate industry context for the individual client's personal sphere. I would have been remiss not to acknowledge that the broader digitization and transformation of the entire death care and estate industry has been accelerated by the pandemic from virtual court proceedings to electronic will creation, remote will-signing, and digital signature capture. Never mind the front- and back-office transformation about to happen in every organization associated with the estate industry. For now, I would recommend getting comfortable with digital assets, as a parlay into what will become a much bigger wave to surf.

Citations

Angus Reid Institute. "What 'will' happen with your assets? Half of Canadian adults say they don't have a last will and testament." *Angus Reid Institute,* January 23, 2018. (angusreid dot org). Accessed February 5, 2021.

Bischoff, Paul. "2/3 of Facebook users haven't assigned anyone to manage their account when they die. Should you?" *Comparitech,* July 11, 2019. (comparitech dot com). Accessed February 5, 2021.

Bruno, Jessica. "How to Report Digital Currency to CRA." *Advisor's Edge*, March 27, 2015. (advisor dot ca). Accessed February 5, 2021.

Cantor, Matthew. "Facebook could have 4.9bn dead users by 2100, study finds." *The Guardian*, April 30, 2019. (the guardian dot com). February 5, 2021.

Card, Jon. "Why tech businesses are tackling society's most taboo subject." *The Guardian*, January 10, 2017. (theguardian dot com). Accessed February 16, 2021.

Caring dot Com. "2020 Estate Planning and Wills Study." and "2021 Estate Planning and Wills Study." *Caring dot Com.* (caring dot com). Both Accessed March 26, 2021. Caring dot com's 2020 survey was conducted in December of 2019 by YouGov. Caring dot com's 2021 survey was conducted in December 2020 by YouGov.

Clitheroe, Paul. "Just over half of Australians adults do not have a will." *Money*, February 18, 2019. (moneymag dot com). Accessed February 5, 2021.

CBC News. "Be cautious about details included in family obituaries, Edmonton police warn." *CBC News*, March 14, 2019. (cbc dot ca). Accessed February 5, 2021.

Consumers Report. "66 Ways to Protect Your Privacy Right Now," *Consumer Reports*, last updated: February 21, 2017. (consumerreports dot org). Accessed February 5, 2021.

CTVNews dot ca Staff. "'Death Cleaning': The new, not-as-morbid-as-it-sounds decluttering trend." *CTV News*, June 25, 2018. (ctvnews dot ca). Accessed February 5, 2021.

Duxbury, Linda and Lanctot, Andre. "Carleton study finds people spending a third of time on e-mail." *Carleton Newsroom*, April 20, 2017. (newsroom dot carleton dot ca). Accessed February 5, 2021.

Elias, Jennifer and Petrova, Magdalena. "Google's rocky path to e-mail domination." *CNBC*, October 26, 2019. (cnbc dot com). Accessed February 5, 2021.

Elliott, Matt. "Two-factor Authentication: How and Why to Use It." *CNET*, March 28, 2017. (cnet dot com). Accessed February 5, 2021.

Francis, Stacy. "Op-ed: More people are creating wills amid the pandemic." *CNBC*, October 5, 2020. (cnbc dot com). Accessed February 5, 2021.

Freeman, Mike. "San Diego's Trust & Will corrals $15 million to expand digital estate planning software." *The San Diego Union-Tribune,* November 17, 2020. (sandiegouniontribune dot com). Accessed February 5, 2021.

Fruhlinger, Josh. "Equifax Data Breach FAQ: What happened,

who was affected, what was the impact?" *CSO*, February 12, 2020. (csoonline dot com). Accessed February 5, 2021.

Genders, Rod, and Steen, Adam. "Financial and Estate Planning in the Age of Digital Assets: A Challenge for Advisors and Administrators," *Financial Planning Research Journal*, Volume 3, Issue 1. (2017). ISSN: 2206-1355 online. (fpa dot com dot au). Accessed February 17, 2021.

Griffith, Eric. "Two-Factor Authentication: Who Has It and How to Set It Up." *PC Mag*, Updated August 4, 2020. (pcmag dot com). Accessed February 5, 2021.

Hartung, Sharon. "How the Internet Broke Estate Planning, Part 1." *American Bar Association*, October 28, 2019. (americanbar dot org). Accessed February 5, 2021.

Hartung, Sharon. "Estate Planning for the Digital Age: Even loyalty points have value when it comes to estate planning." *CareGivers Solutions®,* Winter 2019/20 Volume 21 No 4. (caregiversolutions dot ca). Accessed February 5, 2021.

Hartung, Sharon. "Your Digital Undertaker Attempts To Crack the Code on Death: Getting Your Affairs in Order in the Digital Age." *Death Goes Digital*, Guest Post, September 25, 2019. (deathgoes-digital dot com). Accessed February 5, 2021.

Hartung, Sharon. "Your Digital Undertaker, This is the story of what happens when an IBM delivery leader retires and drags project management and consulting into estate planning." *IBM inTouch*, Issue #51, Fall 2019.

Hartung, Sharon. "Profession: directrice de funérailles numéri-ques, Une chef de la prestation d'IBM à la retraite explique comment on peut utiliser ses compétences en gestion de projet dans la planification successorale." *IBM enContact*, Numéro 51, 2019.

Hartung, Sharon. "Are We Approaching Estate2K for Digital Assets? Three factors on which planners need to focus." *WealthManagement*, Aug. 7, 2019. (wealthmanagement dot com). Accessed February 5, 2021.

Hartung, Sharon. *Your Digital Undertaker, Exploring Death in the Digital Age in Canada*. Victoria: First Choice Books, 2019. FriesenPress: 2019.

Hartung, S., Reich, B.H., and Benbasat, I. (2000). Information Technology Alignment in the Canadian Forces, *Canadian Journal of Administrative Sciences* published by the *Administrative Sciences Association of Canada*, (Vol 17 No4), December 2000, 285-302. ISSN 0825-0383.

Hayes, Molly. "Pressing Google and Facebook for answers in her son's death, an Ontario mother stirs the digital-privacy debate." *Globe and Mail*, August 27, 2019. (theglobeandmail dot com). Accessed February 5, 2021.

Henry, Alan. "The Difference Between Two-Factor and Two-Step Authentication." *Lifehacker*, October 6, 2016. (lifehacker dot com). Accessed February 5, 2021.

Horton, Helena. "More People Have Died by Taking Selfies This Year than by Shark Attacks." *The Telegraph*, September 22, 2015. (telegraph dot co dot uk). Accessed February 5, 2021.

Hu, Jim. "Yahoo denies family access to dead marine's e-mail," *CNET*, December 21, 2004. (cnet dot com). Accessed February 5, 2021.

IDX. "How to Write an Obituary That is ID Theft Proof." *IDX*, April 27, 2017. (idx dot us). Accessed February 5, 2021.

Kasket, Elaine. *All the Ghosts in the Machine: The Digital Afterlife of your Personal Data.* London: First published in Great Britain in 2019 by Robinson, Little Brown Book Group, 2019.

Kemp, Simon. Digital 2020: October Global Statshot. *DataReportal,* 20 October 2020. (datareportal dot com). Accessed February 11, 2021.

Kirchheimer, Sid. "Death Notice Double-Cross." *AARP,* March 7, 2018. (aarp dot org). Accessed February 5, 2021.

Lee, Dave. "Twitter account deletions on 'pause' after outcry." *BBC*, November 2019. (bbc dot com). Accessed February 5, 2021.

Ligaya, Armina. "If you sold or used Bitcoin last year, Canada Revenue Agency wants its due." *Financial Post*, February 1, 2018. (business dot financialpost dot com). Accessed February 5, 2021.

Lumpkins-Walls, Barbranda. "Haven't Done a Will Yet?" *AARP*, February 24, 2017. (aarp dot com). Accessed February 5, 2021.

MacMillan, Amanda. "'Death Cleaning' Is the Newest Way to Declutter. Here's What to Know." *Time*, October 17, 2017. (time dot com). Accessed February 5, 2021.

Mermelstein, Lois D., "KEEPING CURRENT: Ethics Update: Lawyers Must Keep Up with Technology Too." *American Bar Association (ABA),* March 31, 2013. (americanbar dot org). Accessed February 5, 2021.

Michels, Johan David and Millard, Christopher and Joshi, Srishti, "Beyond the Clouds, Part 1: What Cloud Contracts Say About Who Owns and Can Access Your Content." *Queen Mary School of Law* Legal Studies Research Paper No. 315/2019, May 11, 2019. (papers dot ssrn dot com). Accessed February 5, 2021.

Miller, Malinda, "Designing Tech with Mortality in Mind," 2021. CMCI Now Magazine, College of Media, Communication and Information, University of Colorado Boulder. (Engl, Jour'92; MJour'98). Accessed March 23, 2021.

Morgan, Pamela. *Cryptoasset Inheritance Planning: A simple guide for owners*. Merkle Bloom LLC, 2018.

Norris, James. "What is a digital legacy?" and "Digital Death Survey 2018." *Digital Legacy Association*. (digitallegacyassociation dot org). Accessed February 5, 2021.

Olanoff, Drew. "You can take my Dad's tweets over my dead body." *Techcrunch*, November 26, 2019. (techcrunch dot com). Accessed February 5, 2021.

Palmer, Danny. "Windows 7 end of life: Security risks and what you should do next." *ZDNet,* January 14, 2020. (zdnet dot com). Accessed February 5, 2021.

Peckham, Eric. Monetizing Media. Insider analysis on the business of media, entertainment, & gaming. *Monetizing Media*. (monetizingmedia dot com). Accessed February 5, 2021.

Racco, Marilisa. "'Swedish death cleaning' is the latest self-help craze." *Global News,* October 12, 2017. (globalnews dot com). Accessed February 5, 2021.

Ragam, Steve. "Scammers using obituary notices to acquire new victims." *CSO*, February 17, 2015. (csoonline dot com). Accessed February 5, 2021.

Reich, B.H., and Benbasat, I. (2000). Factors that Influence the Social Dimension of Alignment Between Business and Information Technology Objectives, *MIS Quarterly*, 24 (1), 81-111.

Richardson, Danielle, "More than half of parents don't have a will. But what will happen to your children if you die?" *Which?*, December 5, 2018. (which dot co dot uk). Accessed February 5, 2021.

Sagar, Leigh. *The Digital Estate*. London: Sweet & Maxwell, 2018.

Smith, Aaron and Anderson, Monica. "Social Media Use in 2018."

Pew Research, March 1, 2018. (pewresearch dot org). Accessed February 5, 2021.

Tucker, Laura. "Court Determines Spouse Must Be Given Access to Deceased Person's iCloud Photos." *MakeTechEasier,* January 28, 2019. (maketecheasier dot com). Accessed February 5, 2021.

Verde, Tom. "Aging Parents with Lots of Stuff, and Children Who Don't Want It." *The New York Times*, August 18, 2017. (nytimes dot com). Accessed February 5, 2021.

Zegel, Jennifer and Hartung, Sharon. "Five Signs That Estate Advisors Aren't Getting With the Digital Program." *Bloomberg Tax Insight*, July 20, 2020. (news dot bloombergtax dot com). Accessed February 5, 2021.

Zegel, Jennifer and Hartung, Sharon. "Supporting Your Clients' Digital Legacy." *Bloomberg Tax Insight*, April 10, 2020. (news dot bloombergtax dot com). Accessed February 5, 2021.

Citations for the Society for Trust and Estate Practitioners (STEP)

STEP Digital Assets Special Interest Group (Member Reference). "STEP Inventory for Digital Assets and Digital Devices." (step dot org). Accessed February 5, 2021.

STEP Digital Assets Special Interest Group (Member Reference). "STEP Digital Assets Best Practice Guidance." (step dot org). Accessed February 5, 2021.

STEP Digital Assets Special Interest Group (Public Reference). "What Are My Digital Assets?" (step dot org). Accessed February 5, 2021.

Hartung, Sharon. "The digital tsunami." *STEP Journal* (Vol27 Iss4), p.41, May 2019.

Hartung, Sharon and Zegel, Jennifer. "The digital tsunami meets estate administration." *STEP Journal* (Issue 6, 2020), p.66,67, December 2020.

Martin, Kimberley. "Technology and Wills - The Dawn of a New Era - Covid-19 special edition." *STEP*, published August 2020. (step dot org). Accessed February 5, 2021.

Rhoads Perry, Shelley and Hartung, Sharon. "Bolster Your Digital Armoury." *STEP Journal* (Vol27 Iss6), p.50,51, July 2019.

Steen, Adam; D'Alessandro, Steven and Olynyk, Marc. "Estate Planning in Singapore." *STEP* - A research report by the STEP Academic Community, 2020. (step dot org). Accessed February 5, 2021.

Citations for Articles Previously Published in LexisNexis Canada Inc. The Lawyer's Daily

These articles (as quotes, in part or full) listed below by publication date, were originally written by Sharon Hartung and published by The Lawyer's Daily, part of LexisNexis Canada Inc. (thelawyersdaily dot ca). Listed chronologically:

Estate planners: Getting ready for the digital age, Wednesday, August 28, 2019. Accessed February 5, 2021.

Digital privacy for the living and the dead, September 30, 2019. Accessed February 5, 2021.

Digital estate myth#1: All assets are the same, October 8, 2019. Accessed February 5, 2021.

Digital estate myth#2: Hard copy, password managers the answer, October 17, 2019. Accessed February 5, 2021.

Digital estate myth#3: Digital executor solves the problem, October 23, 2019. Accessed February 5, 2021.

Digital assets deep dive: Tech solutions (password managers), November 26, 2019. Accessed February 5, 2021.

Digital assets deep dive: Client management (password managers), December 3, 2019. Accessed February 5, 2021.

Digital asset deep dive: Dangers of ignoring e-mail, December 9, 2019. Accessed February 5, 2021.

Digital asset deep dive: How e-mail affects client's estate, December 16, 2019. Accessed February 5, 2021.

Digital asset deep dive: E-mail for estate planning discovery, January 3, 2019. Accessed February 5, 2021.

Rethinking the obituary in digital age, Jan 08, 2020. Accessed February 5, 2021.

Rethinking the obituary in digital age: Planning and guidance, January 16, 2020. Accessed February 5, 2021.

Windows 7 died without will and estate plan, January 27, 2020. Accessed February 5, 2021.

Loyalty programs, gift cards: Impact on estate planning, February 12, 2020. Accessed February 5, 2021.

Loyalty programs, gift cards: Key points for estate planning, February 19, 2020. Accessed February 5, 2021.

Social media deep dive: Data privacy in death, March 3, 2020. Accessed February 5, 2021.

Social media deep dive: Estate complications, March 13, 2020. Accessed February 5, 2021.

Social media deep dive: Client management, May 8, 2020. Accessed February 5, 2021.

Social media deep dive: Digital details, May 13, 2020. Accessed February 5, 2021.

Digital assets technology awareness: Adapting to change, June 19, 2020. Accessed February 5, 2021.

Digital assets technology awareness: Pivoting to new paradigm, July 3, 2019. Accessed February 5, 2021.

Digital assets technology awareness: Opportunities for estate lawyers, July 14, 2020. Accessed February 5, 2021.

What executors can learn from Quadriga CX: Starting point in discovery, August 7, 2020. Accessed February 5, 2021.

What executors can learn from Quadriga CX: Underlying technology of blockchain, August 21, 2020. Accessed February 5, 2021.

What executors can learn from Quadriga CX: Hardware and software Q1, September 1, 2020. Accessed February 5, 2021.

What executors can learn from Quadriga CX: Technology best practices, September 28, 2020. Accessed February 5, 2021.

Today's Executor is a Digital Executor, October 14, 2020. Accessed February 5, 2021.

Estate tech alignment: Dealing with digital paradigm shift, October 26, 2020. Accessed February 5, 2021.

Estate tech alignment: How IT alignment model works, November 11, 2020. Accessed February 5, 2021.

Estate tech alignment: Which approach suits you best, November 30, 2020. Accessed February 5, 2021.

LexisNexis Three-Part Series, Digital Estate Myths, Accessed December 23, 2020. Accessed February 5, 2021.

Digitization of estate industry: The electronic will changes everything, January 7, 2021. Part 1. Accessed February 5, 2021.

Digitization of estate industry: Table stakes, January 14, 2021. Part 2. Accessed February 5, 2021.

Digitization of estate industry: Five steps to readiness, January 20, 2021. Part 3. Accessed February 5, 2021.

Digitization of estate industry: Five steps to readiness, January 20, 2021. Part 4. Accessed February 11, 2021.

Digitization of estate industry: Starting with one change, February 12, 2021. Part 5. Accessed February 17, 2021.

Your client's web domains: Why more than estate lawyers should care. March 4, 2021. Accessed March 23, 2021.

Your client's web domains: Financial, marketing, sentimental value. March 15, 2021. Accessed March 23, 2021.

Your client's web domains: The mysteries of hosting. March 22, 2021. Accessed March 25, 2021.

Other Corporate and Government Sources:

Note: Service provider terms of service agreements change frequently. Be sure to check for updated information with the service providers of your own digital assets, or for the service provider examples mentioned in this book.

Best Buy, Geek Squad Services. (bestbuy dot com). Accessed February 5, 2021.

Canadian Internet Registration Authority (CIRA). "Canada's Internet Factbook 2020." (cira dot ca). Accessed February 5, 2021.

Facebook. "Managing a Deceased Person's Account." Facebook Help Center. (facebook dot com). Accessed February 17, 2021.

Google. "About Inactive Account Manager." Google Account Help. (google dot com). Accessed February 16, 2021.

Government of Canada. "Unclaimed Balances". (bankofcanada dot ca). Accessed February 5, 2021.

Instagram. "How do I report a deceased person's account on Instagram?" "What happens when a deceased person's Instagram account is memorialized?" Instagram Help Center. (facebook dot com foreward slash instagram). Accessed March 26, 2021.

Internet World Stats. Usage and Population Statistics. (internet-worldstats dot com) Accessed December 23, 2020.

LinkedIn. "Memorialize or Close the Account of a Deceased Member." "Deceased LinkedIn Member." "Request to memorialize or close a deceased member's LinkedIn profile." LinkedIn Help. (linkedin dot com). Accessed March 26, 2021.

Nerds on Site® (Technology Partners). (nerdsonsite dot com). Accessed February 11, 2021.

Twitter. "Request the removal of a deceased user's account." "Request the removal of an incapacitated user's account." Twitter Help Center. (twitter dot com). Accessed March 26, 2021.

Uniform Law Commission (United States). "Fiduciary Access to Digital Assets Act, Revised" (uniformlaws dot org). Accessed February 11, 2021.

Uniform Law Conference of Canada. "Uniform Access to Digital Assets by Fiduciaries Act (2016)." (ulcc dot ca). (2016ulcc0006 dot pdf). Accessed February 11, 2021.

USA Gov. "Unclaimed Money from the Government." (usa dot gov). Accessed February 11, 2021.

Printed in Canada